D0426272

STORIES BEHIND WOMEN *of* EXTRAORDINARY FAITH

Other Books by Ace Collins

Turn Your Radio On: The Stories behind Gospel Music's All-Time Greatest Songs
The Cathedrals: The Story of America's Best-Loved Gospel Quartet
Stories behind the Best-Loved Songs of Christmas
Stories behind the Hymns That Inspire America
Stories behind the Great Traditions of Christmas
I Saw Him in Your Eyes: Everyday People Making Extraordinary Impact
More Stories behind the Best-Loved Songs of Christmas
Stories behind the Traditions and Songs of Easter

STORIES BEHIND WOMEN *of* EXTRAORDINARY FAITH

Bestselling Author
ACE COLLINS

ZONDERVAN®

We want to hear from you. Please send your comments about this book to us in care of zreview@zondervan.com. Thank you.

Stories behind Women of Extraordinary Faith

Requests for information should be addressed to:

Zondervan, *Grand Rapids, Michigan 49530*

Library of Congress Cataloging-in-Publication Data

Collins, Ace.
Stories behind women of extraordinary faith / Ace Collins.
p. cm.
ISBN-10: 0-310-26316-6 (hardcover)
ISBN-13: 978-0-310-26316-6 (hardcover)
1. Christian women--Biography. I. Title.
BR1713.C65 2008
270.092'2--dc22
[B]

2007047655

Interior design by Michelle Espinoza

Printed in the United States of America

08 09 10 11 12 13 14 15 16 • 20 19 18 17 16 15 14 13 12 11 10 9 8 7 6 5 4 3 2 1

To John and Kathy Hillman,
who have used their faith to encourage others
in every facet of their lives

"For I was hungry and you gave me something to eat, I was thirsty and you gave me something to drink, I was a stranger and you invited me in, I needed clothes and you clothed me, I was sick and you looked after me, I was in prison and you came to visit me."

Then the righteous will answer him, "Lord, when did we see you hungry and feed you, or thirsty and give you something to drink? When did we see you a stranger and invite you in, or needing clothes and clothe you? When did we see you sick or in prison and go to visit you?"

The King will reply, "Truly I tell you, whatever you did for one of the least of these brothers and sisters of mine, you did for me."

—Matthew 25:35–40

CONTENTS

INTRODUCTION

Nancy's Faith for Living Each Moment to Its Fullest

Twenty years is a long time. My oldest son was not even in school two decades ago, and now he is a college graduate. My youngest had not been born yet, but enough time has passed that he is in college now. How my life has changed during this passing of time.

Twenty years ago I lost a good friend. At the time she died, she was thirty-three. Thirty-three years is not much time to make a mark on this earth, but she did. And she did it without writing books, starring in movies, or even being elected to office. She made that mark without anyone really knowing her name. Yet the way she lived, that special spirit that could easily be seen in her vitality, joy, enthusiasm, and faith, has inspired me each day since she passed on. And I am not alone. A lot of people are better for having known her, and some might be alive just because of the incredible example she left in her wake.

So I think there is no better place to begin a book on women who possess extraordinary faith than with a personal story of one incredible woman who impacted my life. If you will read this introduction, I think you will find that Nancy will make a huge impact on you as well.

I had a big crush on Nancy when she and I were students at Baylor University, a private Baptist college in Waco, Texas. She had spunk and style that went beyond that of most young ladies in the mid-1970s. Even then I must have realized that all people are special. But Nancy was more special than most. For some indefinable reason, I knew that she was a winner. In every college trial, she proved it over and over again. She was not a person to just play a game; she always played to win. I remember the way she bit her bottom lip when she was hurt or angry. This happened when she made a bad grade on a test, struck out in a softball game, or had a fight with a boyfriend. When she bit that lip, I always knew that she would bounce back.

Fact was, Nancy was no more talented or gifted than other people I knew. She just had more guts, more spirit. In a room filled with people, she stood out. When other people sparkled, she glowed! Yet whenever you were with her, even in a large group, she always made you feel like you were the most important person there. When I graduated from Baylor in 1975, Nancy was the one person I knew who would take the world by storm. Whatever wall she faced, this five-foot-one-inch dynamo would climb it. Whatever goal she set her bright blue eyes on, she would reach. I never had a doubt.

As is so often the case when graduation takes you away to the real world, I lost track of this spunky little lady from Houston. One college homecoming, my wife and I saw Nancy for a few minutes at an alumni coffee. I remember thinking she looked thin. But the moment she turned my way, greeted me with a fire in her eyes and that huge smile, I knew that my college predictions about Nancy must have been right on track. As we talked, I discovered that she was teaching first graders. I couldn't help thinking that those six-year-olds were learning more from Nancy than just how to read. She was making them feel special, filling them with dynamic optimism, and teaching them how to be winners.

Were it not for a chance meeting with her father in the summer of 1985, I might never have made contact with Nancy again. Listening to her father, I began to understand just how high life's walls had been for my college classmate. It was at this point that she began to teach me a profound lesson about living. In that conversation, I discovered that Nancy had spent several weeks at Houston's M.D. Anderson Hospital having a cancerous tumor and infected kidney removed. Weeks of intensive radiation therapy followed. As I listened to her father explain his daughter's battle for life, a picture came into my mind of her biting that bottom lip, gritting her teeth, and facing this painful ordeal with the same determination she exhibited in college. I could see her encouraging the doctors, telling her mother not to worry, and asking her brothers if they didn't have something better to do than hang around a hospital.

Then I found out that there was more to her story than one surgery. Seven years earlier, Nancy and cancer had battled. That war had not been an easy one. Cancer had taken from her an opportunity to have children, but it had proved no match for her strength and spirit. She beat it, knocked it down for the ten count. Cancer had tucked its tail and run to a hiding place. She had won the battle as much with her faith as with her strength. Faith was what Nancy was. It was what she always had been. She believed that God was with her, and she found each test in her life a chance to prove it. If Norman Vincent Peale had needed a poster girl for the power of positive thinking, Nancy would have been it!

After that first battle, cancer hid for more than six years, long enough for Nancy to get the all clear from her doctors. During this time she fell in love, married a wonderful guy, continued to teach, and settled into an active life in the small community of Ennis, Texas. Her energy and enthusiasm for life filled her classroom, her church, and her home. And then, just months before she and her husband, Joe, were to adopt a child, cancer cruelly hit her again. It was after this attack, after that chance meeting with her father, that I once again began to visit with this remarkable lady. Lots of our visits were by phone. But on those rare occasions when we weren't running in five different directions at the same time, we would get together face to face.

During the course of rebuilding our friendship, Nancy lost weight and gained maturity. In personality and determination, she was still the same as she had always been, a person ready to fight the odds to win. She simply knew she would. To her, there was never any question. And just like always, Nancy seemed unimpressed with the courage she had already shown. In her mind, the way she had responded to cancer was just a part of living, a part of who she was. She seemed much more concerned about being at her best when the school year rolled around than she did about the pain caused by cancer and its treatments. In fact, she didn't care if she was weak; she had a job to do, and nothing was going to stop her. As she told me, "I've got kids to teach, so I have to get well fast."

Teaching those kids and starting the school year were the goals that focused her. She knew she had been called by God to teach, and she felt she had to be in the classroom. No one was surprised when on that first day of class, Nancy achieved her goals. She was weak, frail, and probably worn out, but no one would have guessed it.

Over the next few weeks, Nancy had energy in her step and enthusiasm in her voice. In the other teachers' minds, she was simply unstoppable Nancy. This was the way she had always been. Even cancer could not change her attitude. Knowing that Nancy was battling long odds without as much as a single complaint, none of her coworkers could complain about sinus conditions or late hours spent grading papers. She inspired everyone around her to do better than they had ever done before. Never had the Ennis school system worked so well. For a while it seemed like this would be the best year ever in Nancy's young life. Yet for reasons I did not understand and could not comprehend, she simply could not catch a break.

Nancy was able to teach for only a few months before she received another round of bad news. The radiation treatments that had stopped the cancer had damaged some of her organs. More operations were needed, surgery that would alter her diet forever. Most of the foods she loved she would never taste again. Yet she tossed it all off and adjusted her lifestyle. "No big deal!" she told me. And even though all of us should have known better, we tended to believe her words because she said them with such authority.

Even as her faith stood firm, I began to doubt God. Why would he do this to someone like Nancy? Why did she have to suffer so? She was one of life's winners, a leader and a person who inspired everyone around her. In my mind, Nancy's lot in life should have been the easy road, not the path she had been forced to travel.

As my own faith wavered, I asked her if she ever wondered, "Why me, Lord?" Her simple reply will inspire me for as long as I live. She said, "I used to ask that, but then I took stock of my situation and asked, 'Why not me?' If this hadn't happened to me, it might have happened to someone I love. I wouldn't want anyone I know to have to deal with this. God made me strong, so I'll take it. I'll fight it. And I'll beat it."

Her words blew me away. I suddenly realized how much I had been blessed. I immediately applied Nancy's faith and hope to my own small problems and challenges. Through her example, I quickly discovered that life doesn't really have any bad breaks, only opportunities for growth and learning. The more I took this philosophy to heart, the more success I had.

Over the next few months, I stayed in close touch with Nancy. I wanted to watch her handle the rigors of the new treatments. I knew I could learn a great deal simply by watching her take each new step. During one visit she asked me, "Do you remember in college all those times you asked me out and I always had other plans?" I laughed and said yes. "Well," she continued, "if I die before you do, I'll make you one of my pallbearers. Then you'll finally get to take me out." Even as we laughed about that, it never dawned on me that she might actually die. After all, Nancy was indestructible. I honestly believed that after this battle, Nancy would bounce back and assume the breakneck pace she had always maintained.

She almost did.

In late 1986, she took a new test required by the state of Texas for the recertification of teachers. She passed with flying colors. But her celebration was short-lived. She was forced to put off her dreams of teaching for a while longer. Cancer had come calling for a third time. This time it hit her liver. Though she did not admit it, this time I think she knew her time on earth was short. Yet I was still not convinced.

As soon as I found out she was taking on the big C for the third time, I telephoned. Nancy, as always, made me feel like I was the most important person in the world. It was a gift she still had. Nancy and I joked for a while on that visit, then talked about how much we looked forward to things that were coming up. She even told me she wanted to write a book about her life. I assured her that for it to be a best seller, she would have to beat cancer and then do something incredible to celebrate, like run a marathon. Even as I said those words, I knew that Nancy's marathon had already been run and that she had won. I ended our conversation that day by telling her how much my wife and I loved her. She just quietly giggled.

A week later, on a beautiful springlike day, my college crush kept her promise by allowing me to take her out as a pallbearer at her funeral. As I looked around at those at her funeral, I knew I should have felt sadness, but I could not. Maybe it was because her short life showed all of us how to live; her funeral was a wonderful celebration of her wit, her love, and her faith. And because Nancy had made each of us feel singularly special, she had passed on to each of us the secret of her winning edge. Through her selfless example, she had given us the recipe to make others feel as special as she had made each of us feel.

Before she died, Nancy shared these words with a college student who was battling cancer: "Take advantage of everything that cancer has to offer you. It will give you a chance to challenge yourself and find the limits of your strengths and your beliefs. You will have an opportunity to get to know a whole new group of people whose lives are filled with trauma and sadness, and you can bring hope and joy to them by sharing your Christian faith. By getting the chance to fight this disease, you can find out just how special each moment and each person is. Because you will know firsthand what it is like to have it threatened, you will come to a complete understanding of just how sweet life really should and can be. Remember, you can carry the load you've been given, and by doing so, you will help someone else carry his or her load. You have been given the rare privilege, put in the wonderful situation, of being an inspiration. Latch on to this responsibility and give it everything you've got. If you do, you will win!"

Nancy was such a winner. She possessed more life, more heart, and more soul than anyone else I have ever met. But more important, she didn't selfishly hang on to these possessions; she freely gave them all to everyone she touched. Each student, each friend, and each family member felt like Nancy lived only for them, and so they gave back their best to her. She proved that a winner's love never runs out and a winner's touch never ends.

It is hard for me to fathom that twenty years have gone by since Nancy died, but I have no problem understanding why people still remember her. By and large they don't talk about the events of her life; rather they talk about her spirit and how it seems fresher and more alive with each passing day. As a Christian possessing more faith than anyone else I knew, Nancy believed that everyone could touch every moment of life in a good way or in a bad way. She chose the former. I now realize that the sparkle in her eyes, the energy in her step, even the glow of her personality, came not from within, but from on high. As she once told me, "I want everyone to be able to see a little bit of God in me." And we all saw a lot.

To be a woman of extraordinary faith, you don't have to be famous, you just have to live like Nancy lived. And my how she lived!

1

CATHERINE BOOTH

Faith to Stand and Speak

Catherine Booth was a dramatically shy woman who had strong thoughts about faith but chose to hide her convictions deep in her heart. Her journey from quiet woman of faith to the leader of a movement that has touched millions is one of the most remarkable in the annals of Christian history.

On a cold winter day in 1860, a small woman sat uncomfortably in a pew at the Methodist New Connexion Bethesda Chapel in Gateshead, England. Her husband had just concluded preaching to a Sunday morning crowd of over a thousand. On this day, a large number of pastors, some from churches in London, had also gathered to hear the Reverend William Booth present one of his dynamic, uplifting messages. After almost an hour of holding the audience spellbound, Booth offered a prayer and took a seat behind the altar. Most thought the service was over; no one could have guessed that something shocking and revolutionary was about to transpire.

Like many in attendance that day, Catherine Booth had been moved by her husband's words, but as he spoke, she never offered any encouragement with even a quiet amen. She was simply too shy to draw attention to herself in any way. In fact, she was so unsure of herself that she almost always became ill before teaching a children's Bible class. Yet on this morning, she felt the Lord's hand on her back. It was as if he were pushing her forward. Though painfully introverted, she wanted to stand up and speak from her heart, but the rules of the time prevented it. Even the boldest woman was not allowed to stand silently behind the pulpit, much less speak in church, and Catherine was certainly not cut from the sort of cloth that would allow her to voluntarily break convention. Yet in spite of this, she could not remain seated; she had to stand.

Quietly, on unsure legs, she arose and moved to the aisle. Taking a deep breath, the thirty-year-old woman moved unsteadily toward the front of the church. As her confused husband watched, Catherine continued beyond the first row of pews and climbed the steps to where he sat.

"What is the matter?" he whispered as she stood before him.

"I have to say a word," came her reply.

Shocked, William stood, walked back to the pulpit, and announced, "My dear wife wants to say a word." He then stepped back to his chair and, like the rest of the church, waited to hear what Catherine had on her mind.

In a voice so loud and strong it shocked even her, Catherine Booth began, "I dare say many of you have been looking upon me as a very devoted woman, and one who has been living faithfully to God, but I have come to know that I have been living in disobedience, and to that extent I have brought darkness and leanness into my soul, but I promised the Lord three or four months ago, and I dare not disobey. I have come to tell you this, and to promise the Lord that I will be obedient to the heavenly voice."

Catherine continued to address the crowd for several more minutes, then stepped down. As she walked back to her seat, everyone at New Connexion wondered what had gotten into her. Even her husband could not begin to fathom why his wife had chosen this time to speak her mind. Though Catherine herself probably did not grasp the significance, she had just fired the first shots in a revolution, a round of words that would lead to the formation of one of the greatest Christian armies the world has ever seen.

Catherine Booth was able to break down the door that prevented women from addressing men in church only because years of preparation had given her great biblical knowledge and tremendous faith. If she had been born to other parents or in different circumstances, it seems highly unlikely she would have been able to become the most important and influential Christian woman of her time. She fully believed that the experiences of her life had prepared her to be ready to accept God's call at that very moment. Still, she seemed an unlikely woman to make such dramatic church history.

Catherine Mumford was born in Ashbourne, in Derbyshire, England, on January 17, 1829. Her father, John, a coach builder, was a lay preacher and a local leader in the temperance movement. Her mother, Sarah, was a gentle, caring Christian woman who lived her faith through her actions. Sarah treated others with great respect, quoted the Bible as a way of teaching her children life lessons, and attended church every time the doors were open. Catherine was raised in a family much like thousands of others in the England of her day, but a series of seemingly unrelated events would soon set her apart from her peers.

Catherine's mother pressed her to learn in a manner that was more consistent with how the male children of her day were taught. Sarah felt it was important for her daughter to know more than just sewing and cooking, so she arranged for the child to have access to the best works of literature as well as the most recent Bible commentaries. The fact that Catherine was incredibly shy no doubt played into the furthering of her education. She often stayed inside to read rather than go out to mingle with other children her age. In a sense, she was hiding in her studies, using books as a way to escape a world that frightened her. Yet it would ultimately be the knowledge she found in God's Word that provided her with the courage to become a beacon of faith.

By the age of twelve, Catherine had read the Bible through eight times. Before her thirteenth birthday, she was able to quote large segments of Scripture and explain complicated theological doctrine better than her father. Steady and sure in her faith, she dreamed of finding a way to use her knowledge to lead others to Christ. She felt she was on that path when, with no warning, the bottom dropped out of her seemingly perfect life.

Catherine's father's business fell upon hard times. A move to the community of Boston, a port city in Lincolnshire on the east coast of

England, did not turn his fortunes around. Unable to pay his bills, John left his faith behind and, in a move that shocked his family and friends, turned to the bottle. From that point on, John embraced a life that knew few sober moments. He would spend years drowning his woes in what was then called "demon rum."

Her father's fall, coupled with her own insecurities, placed a deep strain on Catherine's fragile spirit. At sixteen, when she moved with her mother to London, she even began to question if there really was a God. For months a sense of panic smothered her. She had problems sleeping, was all but horrified to be awake, and withdrew from almost all activities that took her outside the home. The one consistent social element she continued was going to church. Sitting through hours of worship brought her no solace. In the confines of formal churches, she found no excitement or any evidence of God's Spirit. Though the boring services did not cause her to entirely give up on the idea that God might be alive, she now had no doubt that all the churches she attended were completely dead. At the very moment she was going to give up on practicing any form of Christianity, she happened to read the words of an old Wesleyan hymn, "My God I Am Thine, What a Comfort Divine." Though no sermons had touched her in years and no Bible verses had brought her any peace, for reasons she did not comprehend, the hymn's steadfast lyrics convinced her that God was alive and did care about her. On whether the church was really alive, she still had her doubts.

At the age of eighteen, when she had seemingly fought through her disappointment in her father's fall and her sense of doubt, Catherine was hit by an insidious disease. As it did with millions of others, tuberculosis forced Catherine out of the world and into bed. Convinced there had to be a purpose for her long convalescence, rather than simply sleep her recovery away, she opted to read in-depth articles on the effects of alcoholism on the body. Though she initiated her quest for knowledge as a way to help her father, what she read opened her to the fact that millions were suffering just as John was. She quickly became so alarmed by what she viewed as one of the Devil's strongest weapons, she began to write letters to newspapers and magazines arguing for prohibition laws. Her letters had such a unique slant on the problem that many of the editors requested she expand them into full stories. For a woman too shy even to pray in front of her family, writing gave Catherine a way to voice her knowledge and her passions without fear.

Within two years, Catherine had completely recovered from TB and was looking for purpose beyond her writing. She still believed that God had a special task for her, but she had no clue what that was. Nightly she prayed for guidance and answers, and daily she found neither. Then she attended a Methodist meeting led by an upstart minister named William Booth.

Booth had spent his youth in dire poverty. He had often gone to bed hungry and had few clothes he could claim as his own. He had beaten the odds by learning how to read, but even that education provided him with little upward mobility. His family was thrilled when he landed a job with a pawnbroker, yet Booth quickly grew to hate his work. Day after day, for six long years, he watched men, women, and children come into the store to trade away the last items they owned for a few pennies just to purchase bread or milk. Worse yet were the drunks who pawned their watches or rings to buy another night of alcoholic stupor. As a teen, thirsting for something other than money, he began attending the Wesleyan Chapel in Nottingham. Through the Scriptures, he learned that his vocation stood against what he felt Christ taught. So he walked out of the pawnshop and into the streets to preach to the very people who had once sold him the last valuables they owned. Twenty years old and a charismatic man, he latched onto the Methodist movement and was trained as a roving evangelist. It was in this role that he arrived at Catherine's church.

Booth's views and enthusiasm deeply impressed the quiet Miss Mumford. What he preached was radically different from what the other ministers she had known preached. Booth had no interest in building huge cathedrals or in becoming a pastor to noblemen. In fact, his stance was completely opposite the established views of most local clergymen. William believed ministers should be "loosing the chains of injustice, freeing the captive and oppressed, sharing food and home, clothing the naked, and carrying out family responsibilities." Finally, inside the walls of a church, Catherine had found a man who seemed intent on living out the message she had found in Christ's parables. Naturally, she was drawn to him, but her shyness kept her from rushing up to the man at the end of the service. The two did meet and spoke a bit, but no real relationship was born at that time.

Catherine had always been most comfortable writing her thoughts. So she used letters to compliment Booth on his work and message. When he wrote back, she started to reveal bits and pieces of herself, things she never would have spoken in face-to-face meetings. In the next three years, Catherine and William wrote hundreds of letters. Their correspondence so tied them together that Booth proposed marriage. Surprising many, though she was now deeply in love with the minister, Catherine did not immediately accept.

Catherine had misgivings about some of William's religious views. She had embraced social reform before she had heard him speak. She wanted to find ways to help orphaned children, widows, and even drunken men in the street. Catherine saw this as a direct function of faith and felt that as long as poverty and despair existed, no Christian should rest. What blocked her from saying "I do" was that William always described women as the "weaker sex." He even felt that women should not be allowed to speak in church or to have any say in church business. For months they argued their positions in letters, but neither gave an inch. Finally, Booth agreed that Catherine could address a church if she wanted to, he would not stop her, but he still felt strongly that it was wrong for a Christian woman even to consider speaking out for God in this way.

William's compromise was enough to persuade Catherine to marry him. She felt she had, in a sense, won. What she did not realize was that her future husband had told her she could speak only because he knew she wouldn't. Booth realized that Catherine's shy nature would never allow her to address even a small group of women, much less a large congregation that included men.

On June 16, 1855, at Stockwell Green Congregational Church in London, Catherine Mumford became Catherine Booth. The ceremony was simple and few attended. For their honeymoon, Catherine accompanied William as he continued his speaking tour.

Soon Booth's reputation as a dynamic speaker had grown to the point that the couple's traveling days were over. In 1858, William was named the pastor of Bethesda Chapel, a London church that was part of the Methodist movement. Within months of his appointment, more than a thousand members, from both the lower and upper classes, turned out each week to hear the man's fiery oratory and verbal challenges. Week in and week out, he demanded that his flock become involved in ending the social problems that plagued England. He wanted everyone in his congregation actively living Matthew 25. It was during this time that Catherine, despite her lack of self-confidence, found the courage to teach children.

Since Catherine would still not speak to adult women, William had few worries he would ever see his wife publicly speak of her belief in equal rights for Christian women. Yet on that December day in 1860, everything changed.

Catherine did not know how William would respond to the confusing message she had briefly put forth to the congregation. Over lunch she expected him to ask her to apologize. Yet he didn't. In fact, he looked into his wife's eyes and urged her to explain what had moved her to come forward.

She explained she knew God had given her a message, and she had known it for some time. Yet she had resisted sharing her thoughts with anyone simply because of her introverted nature. As William concluded his remarks that morning, she felt as if she were being pulled from her seat. At that same instant, she heard a voice say, "You will look like a fool and have nothing to say." Catherine suddenly realized that this was the Devil trying to block her from what she had been prepared and called to do. She said she whispered back to that voice,

"That's just the point. I have never yet been willing to be a fool for Christ. Now I will be one."

Impressed, William posed another question: "Where did your courage come from? You have always been too shy to share your thoughts in public. Why now? Why today?"

A now more confident Catherine explained that on one of her recent door-to-door visits to encourage people to come into the church, she had met a young woman living alone in a shack in the slums. This young girl had no food, no water, and no clothes except for the rags she was wearing, but she still invited Catherine in to what were the filthiest quarters she had ever seen. As they spoke, Catherine realized the woman was pregnant and in labor. With no time to get help, the preacher's wife delivered the woman's twin boys. She then raced back home to find clothes, food, and blankets for this new family.

"When I handed her what I had gathered," she explained to William, "I looked into her eyes and saw the Lord looking back. Then, after I came back home and studied the Bible, I noted that it was women who first came to recognize the divinity of Christ. They were the first to display their faith, the first to tell the story, and I realized that women still need to be telling the story today."

Nodding his head, William smiled and replied with yet another question: "What would you like to speak on tonight?"

Not hesitating for a moment, Catherine shared a message that had been placed on her heart many years before. As he listened, Booth nodded. The way the congregation had looked at the tiny woman in church, the way they had hung on her every word as they considered what she was saying had caused the minister to realize that she had not just touched them but had caused them to think. He had thought half the flock might have been sleeping while he was speaking that morning, but they had been very awake when Catherine had shared her short testimony. He wanted to see them stay awake!

That night Catherine presented her first real sermon. Before the service, she was scared to death. When she stood behind the pulpit, her legs were shaking so hard she had to hold onto the wooden structure to keep from collapsing. But after clearing her throat, she boldly charged forward. She read the Scripture passage and then launched into her message on the Holy Spirit's action in people's lives. Some of those in attendance that evening felt sure that lightning would strike her before she had uttered a single word, but when nothing happened, they listened. What they heard seemed to move them in ways William had never witnessed before. In her simple way, with her vast knowledge of Scripture, his wife was causing his congregation to consider what God wanted them to do for the world. When she finished, Booth knew his partner in life was now his full partner in work.

Over the next five years, Catherine found the courage to speak to people in churches, in homes, on the streets, at informal civic meetings, and in schools. She made a habit of going into the streets to visit with drunks and prostitutes. By then a mother of eight, she was dedicated to giving her children a firm knowledge of Christianity through both her words and her example. Yet even as her role in her family and in her husband's church grew, she could not imagine that God had plans beyond what she was doing at Bethesda.

In 1865, William had grown frustrated with regular church work. He felt his role as a minister kept him from his real calling. He gave up his pulpit as well as his regular paycheck and accepted what he sensed was his true calling, ministering to those who lived on the streets and in the slums. With his own funds, he began the Christian Mission, where he preached and provided meals for the poorest souls in London. As he worked with the poor, Catherine arranged to speak to women's groups in the city's wealthiest districts. Day after day she tried to convince those who had been deeply blessed to share a bit with her so she could help her husband reach "the least of these." They needed Christ, she argued, but they also needed food and clothing, and God expected those with funds to share them with the poor.

In today's world, what the Booths were attempting to do doesn't sound radical, but at the time it was seen as a threat to the established British church. Leaders in the Church of England had long been looking for a way to control the radical groups that had spun off, inspired by the teachings of the Wesley brothers. In William Booth they found a poster boy for their cause.

From the pulpits as well as in closed-door meetings, the British establishment began a campaign to destroy the Booths. They put forth the notion that what William and Catherine were actually doing was raising an army of criminals and reprobates to overthrow the Crown and the established church. This was not about religion, they argued; it was about power and the redistribution of wealth. In the press and in pulpits, these men took the Booths' biblical messages and made them look like acts of treason. And for thousands, the greatest sin committed by this pair was allowing Catherine to preach. To much of English society, Catherine's standing in the pulpit as well as addressing men and helping to determine how the mission was run were an abomination to God. After all, she was *just* a woman.

Catherine answered this charge by shouting from pulpits all over London, "If we are to better the future, we must disturb the present." If anyone doubted her convictions, her words proved she was ready for a spiritual fight.

The uproar created by the Booths' trying to reach out to London's poor masses led to William's being arrested and jailed. Behind bars, he urged his wife to carry on the fight. Even though her husband could no longer help her, she was determined to win what she saw as a war against true Christian principles, the rights of the poor, and the rights of women. Though many were now calling her the Antichrist, she continued to hold meetings, distribute food and clothing, and preach.

As she continued to work on London's East End, Catherine remained the organization's leader even after her husband's release from prison. Her preaching had become so inspiring that soon others bolted from normal church services and joined her at the mission. These "converts" usually began their work by handing out food, then went out into the streets to bring more people back for services. To get attention for their cause, they often played musical instruments or sang hymns. Sensing a need to identify her workers as coming from the mission, Catherine made them uniforms as well as flags to carry. Many felt the uniformed groups following the small woman through the streets looked like a small military unit. Because they often were pelted with rocks and peppered with taunts, it would seem they needed some kind of weapon to go with their uniforms, but the once-shy Catherine, now a tower of courage, would not allow any of her band to raise their voices. She urged them to carry themselves as Christ would, even when arrested and jailed.

Within five years of the Booths' founding of the mission, which launched their fight with the established churches, people began to call them and their followers the Salvation Army. The name probably initially was used to ridicule the group, but Catherine liked the label and adopted it. She even declared, "Members of the Salvation Army will fight on, waging war on poverty and injustice wherever we find it."

William added, "The best men in this army are women!" This statement, combined with the encouragement he gave his wife and other women to become equal partners in the ministry, showed how dramatically his thinking on a woman's role in the church had changed since his marriage.

The press, which once questioned the Booths' goals, became the first to recognize the good they were doing. In newspapers, Londoners first learned of the Food-for-the-Million shops, where the poor could buy hot soup and a three-course dinner for almost nothing, of the dinners Catherine prepared for the poor on Christmas, and of the businesses the Booths began that treated workers with respect and provided fair wages and safe working conditions. These stories, along with Catherine's fiery speeches, led women to give money to the same organization their husbands were trying to outlaw. In a very real sense, Catherine's gaining a voice and using that voice to further William's view of what a minister should do ignited a social revolution. Soon, civic and church leaders who opposed the Booths' work began to look like Ebenezer Scrooge.

By 1880, Catherine's army was one of the most respected Christian groups in London and had expanded its work beyond the British shores. The Salvation Army, once feared in London, was welcomed in

New York, Boston, Philadelphia, and every other American city. The woman once too shy even to speak to the man who would become her husband now possessed one of the strongest voices in the Christian world.

Over the last decade of her life, Catherine Booth was openly welcomed by the congregations that had once thought of her and her husband as tools of the Devil. Some of the men who had fought so hard to keep her from speaking in churches became her organization's most ardent supporters. Her army, once ridiculed by the religious establishment, was instrumental in lifting millions of once-hopeless people out of poverty and was viewed as the bedrock of a new revival movement.

Catherine was just sixty-one when she died in 1890. Her son wrote this of her last moments: "Soon after noon, I felt the deepening darkness of the long valley of the shadows was closing around my dear mother, and a little later I took my last farewell. Her lips moved, and she gave me one look of inexpressible tenderness and trust, which will live with me forever. Again we sang: 'My mistakes His free grace doth cover, My sins He doth wash away; These feet which shrink and falter Shall enter the Gates of Day.'

"Holding her hand, the General [William] gave her up to God. It was a solemn and wondrous scene ... the dear General bowing over his beloved wife and companion in life's long stress and storm, and giving her, his most precious of earthly joy and treasure, to the eternal keeping of the Eternal Father. Their eyes met—the last kiss of love upon earth, the last word till the Morning—and without a movement the breathing gently ceased, and a Warrior laid down her sword to receive her crown."

Her death was front-page news everywhere. One memorial story captured her faith, her life, and her legacy with a quote from one of her groundbreaking sermons: "We are made for larger ends than Earth can encompass. Oh, let us be true to our exalted destiny."

2

CATHERINE HICKS

Faith in the Spotlight

As a child, Catherine watched The Donna Reed Show *and realized that she was living in that same kind of world at her own home. She therefore dreamed of creating a home like the one on her favorite TV show and the one she knew in her own house. Little did she realize that as an actress, she would be given a role that would allow her to become America's Mom and that she would get to use her fame to build on her parents' deep faith by touching "the least of these" half a world away.*

In Catherine Hicks' three decades as a motion picture and television actress, she won many awards and was honored scores of times. But the night of September 14, 2006, was much different from any of the other elegant awards events she had attended. On this evening, Catherine wasn't being honored for playing a mom on a television series or a scientist in a box-office smash or as a famous Hollywood film star. She was there because of what she had done under her own name and direction. As the crowd at the dinner in Pittsburgh looked her way, they saw not a celebrity but a woman whose faith drives every facet of her life. In the minds of those who honored her on that night, Catherine Hicks was a person who had embraced and chosen to live the words of Christ found in Matthew 25:35–40 asking his followers to touch "the least of these"—the sick, the hungry, all those in need. For when they did this, that would also be touching him.

The Padre Pio Awards program was a long way in both distance and time from Scottsdale, Arizona, and the 1950s. Yet without her experiences growing up in what was then a sleepy western town, Catherine would never have made it to Pittsburgh. It was in her formative years, as her father's and mother's spiritual examples were being imprinted onto her soul, that the virtues of charity, hope, and compassion were born in this beautiful woman's heart.

In many ways, Catherine was just another child of the post–World War II era. She lived in a safe world. She had a stay-at-home mother, Jackie, who tended to her needs. The family resided in a neighborhood that welcomed bikes, ball games, and hopscotch. Her father, Walter, was a respected local businessman who owned and operated an electronics store. Those who knew him felt he was one of the hardest-working people in the area. Beyond that work ethic, Walter's honesty drove his business practices and shaped his character. He was one of the most respected men in the area.

It's little wonder that in this idyllic environment, one of Catherine's favorite television programs was *The Donna Reed Show*. This thirty-minute drama, centering on the ideal American family, reflected how the girl saw her own life. Week after week, the love, devotion, and goodness Catherine observed on this series reinforced the morality she knew at home. She often dreamed that when she grew up and became a wife and mother, she would reflect the courage, conviction, and compassion she saw dramatized on that ABC show. Little did she realize that just as Donna was a role model for wives, mothers, and children in the fifties and sixties, Catherine herself would become a similar icon in the nineties. Even though she could not see the future, Catherine realized, at a very young age, that it was parents' examples—both good and bad—that provided a lifelong road map for their children.

"I will tell you," she explains, "my mom was from Chicago. She was a fighter, sort of a tough woman, not politically correct. She didn't worry about that; she just spoke the truth."

Beyond her roles as mother and housewife, even beyond her example of honesty in every action and reaction, Jackie presented Catherine with a model of faith. The Chicago-born housewife put God ahead of everything else in her life. She prayed constantly. She prayed at home, in the car, and at church. She prayed both little and big prayers. She believed that every word she prayed was heard, noted, and would be given a response. Nothing could shake her faith.

While it was Jackie who set a pattern for prayer, it was Walter who provided Catherine with an example of action. Walter was not as bold in speech as was his wife; rather, he used his soft-spoken, gentle nature to "sell" the causes that were near his heart. While still in grade school, Catherine observed her father's caring nature in his eyes as much as in his words. The tall, slim man could not ignore the poverty he saw in the dusty community where he lived. It broke his heart to see mothers who did not have enough food for their families or children who were wearing clothes that should have been thrown away years ago. In these needy people, Walter saw his Savior. And so when he was asked to lead a local charity drive aimed at the poorest of the poor, the shy businessman jumped in with both feet. His devotion to this cause made a deep impact on his only child, an impact so lasting that it would someday save thousands in Africa.

"My dad would collect for the Bishop's Relief Fund every year. I grew up in Scottsdale, Arizona, in the 1950s, and people don't believe me now, but back then there was absolutely nothing there but a Catholic church, a few Mexican families, and my parents. And Mom and Dad had moved there from New York City for my dad's health. As the town grew and people became wealthy, Scottsdale became paradise valley, but that is not how it was when I was a child. I remember Dad would collect money to go to missions, like the Indians or the community's very poor people, and he would come back after collecting funds and say, 'You know, the poor Mexican families, the people who have nothing, gave, but the wealthy people always found a reason not to give.' Those words stuck with me."

If Walter had been involved in reaching out just one month a year, then the impact his faith would have had on Catherine's life probably would have been negligible. But the fact that he lived his life giving each and every day, as well as seeing God in every facet of his world, made a deep impression on his little girl.

"The gospel message is so much about giving," Catherine explains. "My father was struggling to survive in Scottsdale, yet he always gave. That is part of being a Christian, giving 10 percent at least. Yet he gave more than money. He gave his time and he gave in the way he viewed the world. My father was a kind human being; he taught me to look at the sunset and thank God for the beauty in it. He pointed out that God's beauty and goodness were all around me. He lived 'Glory, glory, glory to God in the highest.' For him life was always about God. I think he would have been a priest if he had not fallen in love with my mom. That is how deep his faith was."

Catherine learned many lessons from her father, but none had as lasting an impact as the importance of marrying faith to giving. Long before she left home, Catherine had seen Christ staring back at her countless times through her parents' actions.

"Christ was all about giving to the poor," Catherine says. "So many of his words are about that. They are as much about forgiveness and love as they are also about giving to the poor. That stuck in my head, so I got that more from my father and his life than from anyone else."

Besides the love and examples Catherine found at home, she also discovered a deep well of faith at the Catholic church her family attended. The fact that the Hickses were there each time the doors were open provided her with an understanding of how important it was to gather with other believers. She also learned that being in church sent a statement to others and opened a personal window of understanding through worship and prayer. As she grew older, she realized that it was church that grounded her and served as a reminder that being a Christian means more than just wearing a cross or trying to be a good person. It means looking out at a sinful world that doesn't know love, hope, or promise and finding ways to share them in words and actions.

The Hickses also presented their daughter with an example of personal sacrifice by saving a portion of their hard-earned money to send their daughter to Catholic schools. While they realized Catherine could obtain a solid education in the public schools, they felt having a spiritual message constantly playing through the curriculum would provide their daughter with one more Christian tool to steady her when she left their home for the real world.

In school, Catherine saw the constant devotion of the nuns to their work and to the students. The nuns' compassion, prayer, and outreach reinforced what she had already learned at home. "My upbringing, my Catholic education, and my parents—through that influence I came to realize that God was a part of our lives. He was a part of everything, meaning God was just in the air when I went to school and when I was at home."

As an eighteen-year-old high school graduate, Catherine was beautiful, vivacious, dynamic, energetic, and popular. The diminutive blonde had a quick smile and a deep mind. In the middle of a generation that seemed filled with anger, she sensed the wonder of the world, smiled at blessings, embraced rainbows, and looked for positive ways to confront problems around her. She could have gone anywhere to college but chose Saint Mary's in Notre Dame, Indiana, to study theology and English literature. In the midst of trying to find herself and to find a way to use her faith in an unstable world, she discovered a new outlet: acting.

While her first steps in the theater might have been filled with timidity, within a few months she was on her way to being a star. Her obvious talent, along with her incredible beauty, drew rave reviews in college productions. In fact, the only one who seemed surprised when Cornell offered Catherine an acting fellowship to pursue her master's in fine arts was Catherine. Armed with that degree, the former honors student quickly landed a starring role on the network soap opera *Ryan's Hope*. Winning a big daytime fan base was just the beginning. Within a decade of earning her master's degree, Catherine had appeared in scores of movies and television series, playing everyone from a small town girl to Marilyn Monroe. She had even blasted into space on what many consider to be the very best *Star Trek* feature, *Star Trek IV: The Voyage Home*. She was becoming an A-list star.

By the late 1980s, Catherine was always in demand; her schedule was one of the most demanding in Hollywood. Yet even in the midst of her work, she still found time for three things: visiting her parents, praying, and going to church. The glitter of show business might have distracted most people, but the former high school cheerleader's Donna Reed home life had deeply rooted her faith. She was one of the few who never lost sight of the fact that God had made this trip with her. And so hers was a wonderful life that became even more wonderful when she fell in love, got married to a great Christian man, and had a child of her own.

In her role as a mother, Catherine saw the modern world as much different from the one she had been raised in. "One of the things that really bothered me," Catherine says of the industry that made her famous, "was the lack of the spiritual nature of life on TV and in public. I blame the sixties. They [many people of this time] threw out all the good with the bad. A part of the good was religion, and it suddenly was not politically correct to be a part of any organized religion. I am a real mom in the real world, going to soccer games, and I listen to parents who are my age proudly declaring that they are not contaminating their children with any religious preference. I say no, no, that is wrong. Give them something, give them a prayer life, give them a religious tradition. They can reject it later, but if you give them nothing, they have nothing."

In 1996, Catherine was the mother of a four-year-old. She was attempting to provide her own child with the Donna Reed example she had found in her parents' home. But in the materialistic world of entertainment, it was hard to reinforce the lessons taught at home. The family shows of the time didn't seem to present the rewards that come from living an honest, wholesome life. As Catherine prayed for a way to become the kind of parent her own parents had been, another woman of faith was trying to create a modern family show that didn't shy away from presenting positive life lessons.

Veteran television writer and producer Brenda Hampton was born just thirteen days after Catherine Hicks. Ms. Hampton's Baptist faith played into every facet of her life, even as an adult. Brenda was determined to take the success and respect she had earned in 1990s network television to pitch an updated version of the 1950s series that had anchored her childhood. Sensing that the show she envisioned would be greeted with no enthusiasm by the established networks, she turned to a network that was just taking off and badly needed programming.

Hampton's *7th Heaven* was a drama dealing with the problems of a small-town preacher, his wife, and their five children. Realizing the odds were against a series like this finding an audience, Brenda knew she had to find lead actors who were such credible and upright people that fans would believe them in the roles they were to play. The parts of the mother and father had to be perfectly cast. Stephen Collins, who had once considered becoming a minister, was signed as the father. For the mother, Brenda wanted Catherine Hicks.

Surprisingly, when she was approached, Catherine had reservations. She wanted to do more film work, and a series would give her little time to pursue that goal. Yet as she studied the part and saw how the character of Annie Camden reflected so many of her own values, the opportunity became more appealing. Besides, she figured a program like this on a new network wouldn't gain enough of an audience to last more than a season or two. When the run ended, she could go back to doing movies.

Though she didn't fully recognize it during the first few seasons, *7th Heaven* carved out a monumental place of influence for Catherine. As the show's audience grew and fan mail poured in, the actress realized that her portrayal of a Christian mother and wife was making a deep impact. Churches were having watch parties, youth groups were discussing episodes, and the series was revered for bringing mainstream values back to television. Then another door opened up. Media outlets lined up to interview Catherine. Because she played a preacher's wife, she invariably was asked about her own faith. For the first time in her acting career, she was being invited to give her testimony. It was then she realized the incredible gift God had given her in playing Annie Camden.

Unashamed and embracing the same energy she had once used as a cheerleader, Catherine spoke about her Catholic roots, her spiritual parents, and her prayer life. She used her playing of the character of Annie to trumpet the need for Christians to put their faith into action by giving to the world's "least of these." As *7th Heaven* continued into its sixth and seventh seasons, and as the blessings of starring on a successful series brought security to her life, Catherine looked beyond her own church and neighborhood to uncover more ways to live out Matthew 25:35–40. Once again, the childhood lessons of her youth provided her with direction.

Catherine was deeply touched by the film *Hotel Rwanda* and the work of Catholic Relief Services in that area of the world. Though she had been aware of Catholic Relief Services since their work in Kosovo, it was only now that she had the means really to make an impact by sharing her blessings with those in great need in Darfur. It was the images of the dead and dying in that nation that haunted her and drove her to prayer. "My involvement in Darfur is the result of my spiritual involvement in Catholic schools," she explains. "In fact, the nuns, when I was in second grade, made us aware of the poverty in Africa, and we would save our quarters to save African babies. That lesson stuck with me too."

She was driven to learn more about Darfur. Digging deeper, she found that a host of nations were turning their backs on these forgotten people. They were simply letting thousands die each day. Just like her father had discovered when he was trying to raise money for the Bishop's Relief Fund, Catherine discovered that more often than not, the help that was being sent to the area came from the poor and elderly. Knowing the facts prompted a call to action.

Catherine now knew she had to get involved; God wanted her to help, but through what organization? And would just sending money be enough? She made a late-night call to Catholic Charities and asked them about what they were doing in Darfur. She had now found an organization that was doing something to save lives. Knowing her gifts would be making an impact, she opted to take the next step by bringing into play her status as "America's Mom."

Because of *7th Heaven*, millions knew Catherine and trusted her as a role model. Through the media, many of these fans had also discovered that Catherine herself was a woman of faith. By bringing the power of the fictional Annie and the spiritual Catherine together, Ms. Hicks became a loud voice for those in Darfur who had no voice. In print, on radio and television, and even through a special episode of *7th Heaven*, she revealed the extent of the tragedy and provided a vehicle for others to get involved and save lives.

Yet Catherine didn't stop with just one charity outlet. She decided to fully use her Christian voice, as well as her platform as "this generation's Donna Reed," to spotlight other causes. Many of these outreach efforts were not on the other side of the globe; they were just around the corner. To become a Christlike force in Catherine's new missions didn't require anyone to have money.

In person, in print, and through her website, the actress began giving a message to her own baby boomer generation and to their children. Her words sounded like a sermon, and she always delivered them with the passion usually seen in evangelists.

"We will all grow very old very soon, so let us turn our gaze to those who are old now, next door, down the street, in our town, and be kind to them. Don't put it off; start today. Start with a smile, a hello ... chat with them for five minutes as you pass by. They are living, breathing vessels of experience, wisdom, intelligence, and cosmic knowledge. To tap into that resource is to discover a lot!

"It is our mandate as living creatures to care for fellow creatures. Children are cute, animals are fluffy, but old people are often crusty, wrinkly, and slow. But they are so rich in what they know, and they are so in need of a friend. To be old is often to be lonely."

Catherine not only talks the talk, she walks the walk. Giving her money and sharing her fame were simply not enough. She sought out the lonely and offered them her ear and her arms. She also did the same with veterans. She presented this outreach as another way for families and churches to touch the forgotten in their own communities.

"Call your local VA hospital," she begged school and church leaders. "Ask for the chairman of activities. Have your mother-daughter events there and include them in the yearly schedule. Remind your church planners to think of vets at Christmas, Valentine's Day, Memorial Day, and the Fourth of July. Vets are always lonely and in need of a chat."

Putting prayer into action, sharing her physical blessings, boldly speaking out about faith, and using the gift of influence to share God with the world: these are the things Catherine learned as a child. Unlike many, she did not leave the lessons of faith behind when she found Hollywood's bright spotlight. The more famous she became, the more she felt called to be there for the "least of these." It was Catherine's living the lessons taught by her own father that led the Capuchin Franciscan Friars to present her with the Padre Pio Award in 2006. This award, named for a priest who devoted his life to the poor, honors those who live out Matthew 25:35–40. It is presented to the rare few who see Christ in the eyes of the lost and find ways to touch them with faith.

Catherine Hicks grew up to become an answer to her parents' prayers. She matured into a woman of faith who uses her talents to reflect her Christian values. Those who know her are in awe of her giving spirit and deep spiritual beliefs. About the only one who doesn't see what she does as unusual is Catherine.

"That is just the Holy Spirit," she modestly explains. "In a way, I am lucky. I enjoy spending quiet time with God. I love to pray."

A child in Darfur is given a second chance at life, an elderly person in a small Midwestern town gets a visit from two teenagers, and a veterans group in Los Angeles is presented a special program; all these events were set in motion by America's Mom.

"A lot of people ask me what I think is the meaning of life," she laughs. "Well, Christ said, 'Love the Lord your God with all your heart and with all your strength and with all your mind'; and, 'Love your neighbor as yourself.' That's all I am trying to do."

And that's what makes Catherine Hicks not just an extraordinary actress but a great woman of faith.

3

ANNE HUTCHINSON

Faith to Be a Pioneer

Anne stood strong for freedom and faith in both England and the United States. She paid dearly for her convictions, but in the process she influenced the founding principles of her adopted country and inspired millions to follow her lead.

Eleanor Roosevelt was one of the most respected people of her time. She was also one of the first women of the twentieth century to emerge as a major player in world politics. She used her power as America's first lady to expand programs of compassion, charity, and hope all around the globe. Respected for her intelligence and drive, Roosevelt became an icon who inspired a new generation of female leaders. Yet when Roosevelt was asked who was the role model who gave her a road map to speak up with a confident voice in a man's world, the first person she pointed to was an American pioneer. In Anne Hutchinson, Roosevelt saw the emergence of the first American foremother. As a woman, Anne Hutchinson stood tall while men shrank from this established figure of authority. She commanded respect even from those who felt her views were too radical to embrace. A woman who came to America to seek religious freedom, she ultimately set in motion a movement that would guarantee that right in this new world. And in that process, she opened the door to both men and women having a meaningful one-on-one relationship with their Lord. By grace Anne Hutchinson presented a faith so deep that the movement continues to this day.

In the early 1600s, men and women all over Europe were excited by the prospects of living in a land where they could worship as they felt God called them to do. Many whose faith had been oppressed in their own countries saw the New World as a place where the Word was alive and available for the masses. It was an exhilarating time to be a Christian, an era that seemed to finally fulfill the promise of the faith Christ presented to those who knew him when he walked on earth. Sadly, in the midst of this great new era of hope, there was a faction demanding debate and stirring controversy and anger. Many wanted to limit the study of faith to a select few church leaders. Almost all men of the time felt that women had no place in formal worship or Bible study. In their limited view, God did not use women or speak to them. Thus, even in the New World, Old World ideas prospered.

Into this mix of complex and controversial views of faith, in the summer of 1591, was born Anne Marbury in Alford, Lincolnshire, England. Anne was the daughter of Francis Marbury, a leader at Christ Church in Cambridge, who would become the most dynamic role model of Anne's early years, a rebel with a cause. He believed the established church had degenerated into a political organization, with ministers assigned because of their powerful connections rather than their ability to serve. Marbury saw these undedicated clergymen as an affront to the gospel and actively spoke out against what he felt was a process that was killing the Christian movement in England.

As was to be expected, Marbury was arrested and tossed in jail for speaking against church leaders. Labeled a subversive for his campaign to take the church out of the hands of the state and place it back into the hands of God's people, he became an outcast. Still, he found supporters for his cause, though they were few in number. Eventually he rose to the rank of rector at St. Margaret's Church. Rather than mellowing in his new position, he boldly spoke against churches that did not put their congregations and Christian service before loyalty to powerful church leaders.

Anne, who idolized her father, was not, as a female, allowed to attend local schools. So her father taught her at home. He encouraged his daughter to question everything she read, and she did not hesitate to do so. Marbury also demanded that his daughter think, even challenging the girl to give her views on what God meant to her and how he wanted to use her during her life. This kind of thinking was unheard of in the early 1600s, but because of this type of education Anne developed a deep interest in religion and theology. It was an area most women of the time were not allowed to speak of, much less study. It was this facet of her education, as well as the example set by her father's bold view of the work of the church, that created a dynamic situation where Anne would become the first woman to stand as an independent force of Christ in the New World.

At the age of twenty-one, the outspoken and assertive Anne married a man she had known since childhood. Will Hutchinson had also been educated by Anne's father and was a member of a family that headed a flourishing textile business. Thus, like his wife, he was a liberal thinker when it came to matters of faith, but because of his position in the business world, he had the power to express himself freely.

Will was a man far ahead of his time in matters of women's rights. He not only valued his wife's opinions on matters of faith and business, he asked for them. Anne was very much an equal in every facet of their marriage. While she may have fully embraced her role as a wife and mother, this new bride did not give up her interest in theology. Excited by the prospect of women becoming a vital part of the emerging Protestant movement, she became fascinated by the teachings of John Cotton. Cotton's viewpoint that grace rather than works paves the way to salvation was similar to Anne's father's view. This belief was becoming popular in the Puritan movement and seemed to empower men and women to work together in God's world.

Cotton, and many others like him, wanted to instill an active and vital form of faith that mirrored what they saw in Christ's interaction with people during his time on earth. They felt churches should be governed locally, independent from corporate control. They held that pastors should watch over their flocks like a shepherd, making decisions based on individual needs, not on an edict from a person they had never met. Some even saw the role of women as being substantial and important in the new church. They argued that it was women who were among the first to recognize the divinity of Christ; thus history had established women to be vital in the emerging modern church. Some even suggested women could serve in a variety of leadership roles. Though Cotton did not go so far as to suggest a woman could speak for God in front of a congregation, he did gladly instruct women and saw them as valuable independent thinkers. One of his prize pupils was Anne Hutchinson. He encouraged her to debate and constantly praised her biblical knowledge.

Anne enjoyed Cotton's classes because it gave her a sounding board for her ideas of faith. She fully embraced the right of women to be able to speak out if called. She felt a need to take Christianity back to its roots by tearing down the walls separating men and women from direct communication with God. She was even bold enough to tell friends and neighbors that she spoke directly to her Lord in prayers and did not feel the need to go to a pastor to interpret the meaning of Scripture. She trumpeted the fact that she had a very personal relationship with Christ and she believed that is what the Lord wants for all men and women. Anne's viewpoint would have been considered heresy by most Christians of that era, but her husband and preacher did not ask her to refrain from expressing her beliefs.

Anne Hutchinson, who had given birth to fifteen children in her first twenty years of marriage, was usually too busy with household chores to express her radical viewpoints in public. Yet at the heart of her personal conversations always echoed the belief that faith was the most important element of being a Christian. She argued that she had been saved by grace, and that once she had been saved, God would always be in her heart. She further believed that his grace was all she needed to get to heaven. She scoffed at the then-accepted concept that any person could be saved by works. In her mind, works paled in comparison to grace. She pointed out that grace was what Christ had tried to give to all those he met during his walk on earth. She enjoyed noting that generally it was the women of the Bible who first picked up on this concept.

Even after the Reformation, being saved by grace was not the established viewpoint of the Church of England. It was a discouraged Anne who found that the new church movement still largely embraced the old church ideas of works being more important than grace and faith. Eventually this unbending doctrine caused her (as well as thousands of others) to look beyond her native land to a new world for hope.

In 1633, after being arrested several times for his radical views on faith, John Cotton left England for what he hoped would be a more liberal America. Losing Cotton was a huge blow to Anne. He had been her teacher and mentor; without him she had no one outside her home to engage in discussions of theology and church doctrine. Soon after Cotton departed, two of Anne's daughters were taken by the ravages of the bubonic plague. In her grief, Anne grew more and more despondent. She felt as though in her native land she had no hope. Sensing the oppression that railed against religious freedom in England would not weaken, she began to search the Bible for strength and direction. While studying Isaiah she came across a verse that read, "And though the Lord give you the bread of adversity, and the water of affliction, yet shall not thy teachers be removed into a corner any more, but thine eyes shall see thy teachers" (Isaiah 30:20 KJV)

Knowing she could never again see her late father or bring her children back from the grave, and realizing that John Cotton was also never coming back to England, Anne began to talk to her husband about moving to America. In her prayers she had been given a vision that she could make an impact for her Savior. She was sure America was a land where grace would be accepted and would flourish. Will listened to his wife's wishes, considered his own future options in England, and opted to seek adventure rather than hold on to security. Selling his business and their home, he purchased passage on a sailing ship, the *Griffin*, and bought the items needed to sustain his family in the Massachusetts Bay Colony. Surely in this new land, he reasoned, men and women would be much more open in their theological thinking. Sadly, the Hutchinsons would soon discover the opposite was true, and it would be his own wife who would pay the greatest price for this leap of faith.

The reunion with her former teacher on the shores of the New World proved anything but happy for Anne Hutchinson. America had dramatically changed John Cotton. He had become the dictatorial voice for his congregation. He and the church elders had decided they spoke for God and no one dared challenge them. When Anne and Will attempted to join Cotton's church, he demanded she confess to being "guilty of wrong thinking." In other words, in Cotton's classes in England she had acknowledged that works were secondary to faith and that a woman had a right to interpret Scripture. Now she was expected to distance herself from her beliefs. Anne confessed to being a sinner, but she carefully did not acknowledge any error in her thinking. At the time she thought she could adapt to the rules of the Massachusetts Bay Colony. She was greatly disillusioned by the man who had left England because of religious oppression, but now was determined to oppress anyone who did not conform to his biblical views. For Anne, who hoped for a life filled with grace, this New World seemed much more like the old one.

Initially the dictatorial thinking of the Puritans in the Massachusetts Bay Colony drove scores of progressive men and their families to other parts of the New World. The Hutchinsons moved in next to John Winthrop, the local governor. But both Anne and Will wondered how long they would be welcome in this community of narrow-minded believers.

What Anne quickly discovered was that under Winthrop's and Cotton's leadership, everyone was free to worship as long as they did not think while they were worshiping. If anyone, outside of the men who ruled the church, questioned any facet of church work, they were called up and asked to confess their sins against God. Never had Will or Anne felt as stifled.

In a move that would set a model for generations of American women, Anne quietly rebelled. Setting up Bible studies in her own home, she explained to scores of women the meaning of the Scriptures used in the church during the previous week's sermon. At her home, women who had been brought up to feel inferior to men in mind and body were challenged to consider what their heart told them about their faith. They asked Anne questions, began to study the Bible on their own, and even dared speak up and ask their husbands about matters of church and state.

Over the next two years, Anne's weekly meetings became so popular that even men began to attend. They listened to the teacher's viewpoints on Scriptures and took a great interest in her view of faith being more important than works. Over time Anne's ideas created so much discussion in the Bay Colony that she had to hold more than one class a week.

Though the meetings were not advertised, John Winthrop could not help but notice, from the front window of his home, all the activity. As these meetings grew more popular, the governor began to sense a certain degree of empowerment coming from the area women. When members of Anne's class asked the church to have a copastor, one who embraced the importance of faith in salvation, the governor began to feel threatened. As Anne's influence grew, Winthrop sensed that she had become the most dangerous person in New England. Far from giving up the ideas she had expressed to Cotton in England, she had brought them with her and was now sharing them with others. If she was not silenced, Winthrop feared the ruling class would soon lose both control and power.

After discussing his feelings with others in the church, Winthrop demanded that Anne stop her weekly study and prayer meetings. He told Anne, in front of the church body, that these gatherings "are a thing not tolerable nor comely in the sight of God, nor fitting for your sex." He further stated, based on Puritan biblical views traced back to Eve, that a woman who learned to think was a woman who would soon embrace sin in every facet of her life. Having women discuss biblical matters and form their own ideas on the lessons found in the Good Book would lead to the downfall of the entire Christian community. Winthrop's words sent such fear throughout the colony that many women burned their diaries rather than have anyone believe that they had an original thought. Yet the group's leader stood strong.

In defiance of the governor, Anne continued to teach, but her classes were smaller. Those who now gathered to hear her thoughts were only the bravest men and women in the area. Not satisfied that he had quelled the danger to his rule, Winthrop ordered the classes shut down in the summer of 1637. To strike fear into the hearts of those who might ignore his words, he sent armed guards to arrest Anne. He ordered that her teachings be examined, and if it was found that she had blasphemed the church, she would be put on trial. Though a committee was formed to rule on the content of Anne's meetings, the committee was largely for show. Winthrop ultimately determined that the forty-five-year-old pregnant woman would face judgment. Even before he put her on trial, Winthrop called Anne Hutchinson "an American Jezebel, who had gone a-whoring from God." He then demanded the church leaders decry her as a heretic.

Officially, Anne was accused of committing the crime of antinomianism. This meant she held the belief that Christians were liberated from the observance of moral laws when God's grace is active. Specifically she was damned for believing that an inner light, as per experiencing the Lord in one's soul, was the guarantee of salvation. It was Winthrop's argument that teaching a man or woman that they did not need to follow specific Puritan edicts, rules, and doctrine to be saved was an admonition against God and the church. Thus, Winthrop declared Anne, like Eve, was in league with Satan.

The church leaders who studied her teachings in preparation for her trial found a great deal morally wrong in her thinking. Anne believed that each person should dictate what was right or wrong as God directed them to believe, not as was written in church laws. Embracing this concept of free spiritual thinking, she taught that Indians were God's people and should not be oppressed into slavery. She also felt the Massachusetts Bay Colony had no right take the natives' land without proper payment. She taught that each Christian could approach God as an individual.

Anne was not alone. A number of men and women supported her views. For Winthrop the problem was not so much with her beliefs as with her charisma that pulled this faction together into a group that might challenge the establishment. She was viewed by the governor and others as a rival to their power. The best way to bring her down, they decided, was on moral grounds. As Anne would soon discover, truth would take a backseat to lies, as her innocent meetings of faith would be portrayed as orgies of sinful activities.

After several months of gathering evidence, the trial began in November. With no lawyer, Anne stood in front of a panel of forty-nine well-educated men, the wealthiest men in the colony. In truth, she had no chance but to throw herself on the mercy of the court and beg for their forgiveness. Though sick, cold, and nearing the time for the birth of her child, Anne Hutchinson refused to back down. Her fight might not be one she could win, but she would never renounce her belief that Christ came to offer grace and salvation to all who believe.

John Winthrop, who by this time deeply hated Anne Hutchinson, assigned himself as lead prosecutor. As per English law, Anne was viewed as guilty unless she could prove herself otherwise. As cold winds blew outside, the governor detailed eighty-two different laws the defendant had broken. He forced the frail woman to stand for hours as he lambasted her with charges. She might have collapsed in fatigue, which would have caused the proceedings to be delayed, but she showed no signs of backing down.

After Winthrop's opening, the panel's initial questions were easily answered by Anne. As she showed her understanding of the Bible, some hostile church members softened their view of the woman. Many began to see her as the most knowledgeable spiritual authority in the room. Some even predicted that Anne would prove herself innocent and be set free.

Anne might have won the trial if she had compromised her beliefs. All she needed to do was submit to authority, bow before her accusers, and agree that as a woman she had little worth in God's worldly plan. But Anne would not do that. When challenged, she fought back. She proudly uncovered the areas where the church leaders were showing bias or inconsistent thinking. When she got a chance to make someone look foolish, she did. In time her attitude even angered her former teacher.

John Cotton could have come to her defense. He knew her heart and had once taught many of the principles that led to her belief in grace and faith. Instead, the preacher lashed out in words that may have even shocked Winthrop. He called Anne's meetings "a promiscuous and filthie coming together of men and women without Distinction of Relation of Marriage," an implication that sex was the goal of these gatherings. He added, "Your opinions frett like a Gangrene and spread like a Leprosie, and will eat out the very Bowells of Religion."

Over the next few days each of the church leaders, as if possessed, took the opportunity to verbally attack Anne Hutchinson. Knowing now that if they quoted Scripture she could fire back with theological arguments that usually trumped theirs, they pulled the battle down into the gutter. Time and again they accused Anne of stepping beyond her role as a Christian woman. They demanded to know what gave her the right to teach men and to challenge the male leaders of the faith.

With no hesitation, Anne told the court that God had directly spoken to her on many occasions, "by the voice of his own spirit in my soul." She heard him when she prayed. It was he who had sent Jesus, and through his death she had been offered salvation by grace. Therefore the rulings of the court and these men were moot because only God could judge her.

Though she had little chance even before the proceedings began, her stand that women were equal in the sight of God spelled her doom. Many fully expected the court to put her to death. Fearing retribution if she were to be burned at the stake, the court ruled Anne would be banished from the Bay Colony after she had given birth to her child and both were well enough to travel. Until that day she would remain under guard.

In the spring of 1638, the Hutchinson family, along with sixty others who believed in what Anne had taught, left the Puritan-controlled areas and departed for the freedom of Rhode Island. Anne lived out her years in exile, first in Aquidneck, Rhode Island, and later on Long Island. In September 1643, during an Indian attack, she and her family were killed. Yet Anne Hutchinson's fight for what she called the covenant of grace was not forgotten nor did it die. Her passion was adopted by a host of others, including Roger Williams. In fact, it was the Puritans' trial against Anne that, more than a century later, was considered one of the primary factors in the establishment of Article VI of the Constitution. Some even thought of this segment of America's greatest document as a memorial to her courage and faith. No doubt Anne would have appreciated the wording that "no religious test shall ever be required as a qualification to any office or public trust under the United States." She would have also taken comfort in knowing her cause was again remembered in Article I of the same document: "Congress shall make no law respecting an establishment of religion, or prohibiting the free exercise thereof." It was at least in part Anne's stand that led to the founders of the United States being guided to enact religious freedom as the rule of the land. And it would be this governmental covenant that would make America a beacon of religious freedom for the entire world.

Eleanor Roosevelt, as well as scores of historians, have long considered Anne Hutchinson as America's first great female leader. Yet Anne may have been more than just the first of her gender to stand up for her rights as an American Christian; she probably was the voice that set forth the salvation-by-grace-and-faith movement that would one day sweep this new land. God used Anne Hutchinson to create a brave new world of hope and grace at a time when most didn't believe the Lord ever used women.

4

MARGUERETE SMITH

Faith to Share

Marguerete represents millions of Sunday school volunteers who for two centuries have cared enough to give their best and in the process have fulfilled the Great Commission like few others.

Throughout the late 1770s, Robert Raikes, the owner and editor of the *Gloucester Journal*, used his paper to point out the plight of poor, uneducated children who often worked long hours in subhuman conditions throughout the British Isles. These children were treated no differently than beasts of burden. They received little for their hours of hard labor, were often abused, and lived in appalling conditions. Riddled with disease and parasites, usually wearing the only clothes they owned, many died well before they reached their teens. Those who were lucky enough to survive their childhood were hardened, sullen, streetwise criminals who preyed upon the weak and helpless. The gangs they formed owned neighborhoods and struck terror in the hearts of even the most veteran English policemen.

Raikes saw these bands of ragged youths not as hopeless trash, but as God's children. The journalist did not want them put in prison; he wanted them educated and given an understanding of the basic moral concepts that had so enriched his own life. Yet most of society did not share his vision. When local authorities turned a deaf ear to his request for government intervention and local churches failed to act on this problem, Raikes took the matter into his own hands. In 1780, in Sooty Alley, Gloucester, in a building opposite the city jail, the cheery, talkative, flamboyant, and warmhearted Raikes started a new type of Sunday morning worship service. His building was open only to street ragamuffins, and those who ventured inside were treated with respect as they listened to the publisher share the great stories of the Bible.

Word quickly spread throughout Gloucester, and boys of all ages began to visit the Sunday morning Bible school. For many it was the first time they had ever heard about Moses, Noah, and Jesus. The message of those early-morning meetings, combined with the compassion and love given to them by Raikes and his volunteers, had a dramatic effect on the children and on the community. Crime rates sharply declined as many of the hardened young criminals were transformed into model citizens.

The news of Raikes' success quickly spread across the British Isles, and in 1785, the Sunday School Society was formed to develop the work and export it throughout the United Kingdom. Within a decade, tens of thousands of boys were attending Sunday schools in almost every major city and village in England, Scotland, and Wales.

As Raikes' inspiration caught fire, a dynamic author, a woman, was responding to a call to establish homes and schools for impoverished girls. After observing the effects of Sunday schools on boys, she expanded her vision to include a Sunday school for girls in Mendip Hills. For many of these young women, it was not only the first place they ever heard stories from the Bible but also the forum that allowed them an opportunity to learn to read and write.

Sensing its international potential, Hannah More became a spokesperson for the movement, urging churches to take up the concept of Sunday school. She first convinced a wing of the English Methodist movement to get involved, then other denominations followed. By the early 1800s, thousands of churches, which in the past had offered no type of regular religious education for children, were seizing on the vision of Raikes and More as if it were their own.

Even as More watched the movement expand around the globe, she couldn't have fully realized the impact Sunday school would have on millions. This radical concept, set up at a time when many children were not even offered a public education, did more than just save millions of forgotten street children, it also served as the launching platform for thousands of preachers, teachers, missionaries, and social activists. It would mark the beginning of a Christian outreach not before seen in the industrialized world. Yet the model that More sold to churches was unique because it depended on Christian volunteers to make it work. As More put it, "If faith produce no works, I see / That faith is not a living tree. / Thus faith and works together grow, / No separate life they ever can know. / They're soul and body, hand and heart, / What God hath joined, let no man part."

One hundred and fifty years after the Sunday school movement began, the Sunday classes had become commonplace. They were as much a part of Christian life as hymns and sermons. Yet the enthusiasm that seized so many when More spoke in churches about establishing these beacons of hope and faith was beginning to dim. It was becoming harder to convince men and women to teach classes every Sunday morning. In a day when gangs of children no longer terrorized city streets, many saw little value in volunteering to teach old Bible stories. Of those who did accept the calling, few took the role as seriously as had Hannah More—except for a teacher in East Texas, who saw Sunday school as more than just an hour of Christian daycare. This woman, whose classes never numbered more than twenty, inspired scores, including a Grammy-winning singer, and set a model for Sunday school teachers everywhere.

Every Sunday morning for as long as anyone could remember, a few hours after the East Texas sun had begun to pierce the dense piney woods, men, women, and children, all dressed in their best clothes, would leave their homes and head for a small rural church. In a dusty clearing just down the road from the tiny community of Gary, a frame-and-brick building surrounded by tall trees stood waiting for them. This small church had seen countless services, hundreds of weddings, scores of revivals, and a host of Bible study sessions. Through its modest doors new members had been welcomed and old friends had been remembered, Scripture verses had been learned, and the fabric of life had been revealed. It was more than a church—it was a place of gathering, a place of learning, a place of joy, a place of hope and love.

To the farm families who made up the membership, this was much more than a building. It was a home.

For many people in this rural area, the church had long been a vital part of every facet of their lives. The creaks in the floor, the feel of the pews, the worn pages of old hymnals — these were all friendly elements that made worship a more intimate experience. In many cases, the children who were rocked in their parents' arms during long sermons grew up and married and saw their own children married and eventually died without ever moving their spiritual home away from Enterprise Missionary Baptist Church. City congregations may have had fancy choir robes, huge budgets, and tall steeples, but this small church could lay claim to members who were as honest as a Texas summer day was long. These people were the salt of the earth.

There was rarely a time when the building's old wooden doors were open that the Davis clan wasn't there. Like generations before them, these were people of great faith. Their love of the Lord was as deeply rooted as an East Texas pine tree. They believed in the importance of worship. They had always brought their three children to the Lord's house to firmly ground them in a strong foundation of faith. The family knew that their God was the one true God, one who would never forget them, and one who would always deserve their respect.

Linda, their youngest daughter, was a big-eyed, long-legged junior high student. She thought of everyone at this church as family. In fact, most were either her kin or neighbors. Yet even those rare folks who moved into the area were quickly welcomed into the circle. These people harbored deep convictions and great love, and they freely shared in every member's pain and joy. Like thousands of other small, simple congregations, they loved life, ignored hardships, and considered themselves fortunate to be able to live where they lived and to have the modest possessions they had. Through song, prayer, and Bible study, they challenged each other to be the best they could be. They were the product of the pioneer spirit of their parents and grandparents, and they were role models for future generations of Christians growing up under their watchful eye. Though far from perfect, they were what the people of a church were supposed to be.

Even on days when Linda was tired or didn't feel well, even when the weather was terrible, even when there was nothing going on that interested her, she was expected to go to church. There were no choices or excuses. The simple act of going despite anything and everything was a sign of the importance her family placed on faith.

"I can't deny," Linda remembered, "that a lot of times I felt like I was made to go and that was kind of a bummer. But I wouldn't take anything for those days and that time. I loved the people in the church, and they loved me. They were interested in my life, and I could feel their concern and see their devotion. It was a family, and I could depend on that family."

So each Sunday, rain or shine, Linda would get out of the family car, greet those out in the parking lot, wave to her friends, and duck in a side door that led to her Sunday school room. It was the same routine each week, and there was a certain security and comfort in it. But one morning, just after she had begun seventh grade, something was different. The kids in the room were still the same, but the teacher was someone she didn't know. For a second it threw her off. Linda shyly took a seat across the room from this new face, all the while looking down at the floor and trying to not be noticed. As the other kids whispered quietly to each other, Linda nervously looked up. When she did, her gaze met the warm, deep eyes of an older woman. Linda's first instinct was to glance back down to the floor, but for some reason she didn't, and this action was rewarded with a big smile.

"I'm Mrs. Smith," the petite gray-haired woman offered. "My husband and I moved out to the lake. We're from Dallas."

Nodding her head, Linda forced a smile and replied, "I'm Linda Davis.

"It's nice to meet you."

Linda didn't know it then, but this happy, lively, middle-aged Sunday school teacher would have a profound effect on her life. Their hearts and minds would bond, and suddenly years of memorizing

Bible verses and learning songs would give way to real understanding of both herself and the Lord.

"On the day that Mrs. Smith first came to teach us," Linda recalled, "there were about eight or nine kids in the class. None of us was prepared for what we were about to experience. We just figured that this was just another person who would teach us and relate to us in the same way that all the other teachers had. But she was different. She was the first adult who seemed to know and care what was going on in our world. She didn't expect us to come up to her level—she came down to ours.

"As the morning moved on, she took verses that had seemed boring and brought them to life. She tied them into things that were a part of our lives. She made them seem important and relevant. She just had a refreshing way of introducing us to the Bible. She made it challenging, she made it interesting, and she applied it to where we were. I had never met anyone like her. Instantly she was more than a teacher, she was a friend and a member of the family. I just loved her from the very beginning."

Suddenly, Sunday was a whole new adventure. Linda was now the first one up, the one dragging her folks to the car, exploding into the classroom, babbling about the lesson, and talking about it with her friends. Now each Sunday was a time to look forward to, and Linda no longer wished she could sleep in. Mrs. Smith's influence as a teacher and her witness as a Christian didn't begin and end with the Sunday school bell.

Loading the kids in her car, there were Friday night excursions to Mexican cafes, putt-putt golf courses, and movies. Some weekends there were cookouts at her house and long evenings spent fishing on the lake. And for Linda, whom the childless woman had taken a great shine to, there was more.

"Even though she taught a group of us," Linda explained, "she genuinely cared about us as individuals. She wanted to know what was going on in our lives. In some ways it was like she was our age. She was a friend. It was kind of funny. Here she was, as old as if not older than most of our parents, but after a while she seemed like she was as young as we were. Her love and understanding transcended the years.

"I was the only one at my house at that time—my brother and sister were older and they were on their own. The Smiths would invite my dad to come over and use their boat to go fishing, and I'd go along and spend the afternoon with Mrs. Smith. I guess I spent more time with her away from the church than the other kids in class. I just loved her. She was so positive. I believed then, and I still believe now, that she lived like a Christian was supposed to live. She didn't say anything bad about anyone. She cared about folks and tried to understand them, and she was so sensitive that she could always tell if you were hurting.

"Sometimes it's hard for an adult to deal with a kid in junior high. That's such an awkward age. You spend a lot of time going up and down, and you just don't fit in anywhere. But at her house I felt like I was perfect. She made me feel like I was mature and confident, that I could do anything. She did a great deal for my self-esteem, which in turn did a great deal for my understanding the power of being a Christian."

Being a Sunday school teacher at any level is a job that many people avoid. Having to prepare a lesson, try to find new ways to address old subjects, and get up and be excited every Sunday morning is tough. Many times the students are bored and the time invested in study seems wasted. Being a teacher assigned to a junior high class is often looked at as combat duty. Most people don't just avoid this age group—they run from it.

Despite the fact that she was new to the area and new to the congregation, Marguerete Smith didn't run away when asked to handle the toughest age group in church. Rather, she snapped up the opportunity, grabbed the materials, and dedicated herself to doing her best. As a student of the Bible, she must have been aware that Christ got down on the level of those he met. He didn't address them from up on a throne. He walked with them, ate with them, laughed with them, and comforted them. He didn't demand; he encouraged. It was obvious that

Mrs. Smith used her Savior as her role model. And in Linda Davis's case, she made quite an impact.

"One of the things I remember so well," Linda explained, "was that she always found the good in things we did. She could always find a way to compliment what we had done. Even if something I made didn't turn out right, she would see an element she really liked in it."

A bright student, a cheerleader, a popular girl, Linda was involved in a lot of different activities, and Mrs. Smith seemed to be able to keep up with them all. More than anything else she did, Linda loved to sing. Her voice was powerful, and whether it was performing a solo in church or singing with a local country band, Linda Davis was getting more and more attention.

"Some of the folks thought my singing at local shows and stuff was wrong," Linda remembered. "They thought I should only sing in church or at school. As I began to travel over to Ft. Worth and other areas that were a long way from home, I would miss church some. Yet Mrs. Smith never discouraged the country music direction, and I appreciated that. Unlike some of the others, she never judged me. As a matter of fact, she told me that I was doing a great job of using the talent the Lord had given me."

As Linda grew up, she spent more and more time singing at shows. Although this prevented her from seeing as much of Mrs. Smith, they kept in touch, and Linda knew that her teacher understood her absences. Then, just before she entered the tenth grade, Linda found out that the Smiths were moving. On one of her final visits, this woman who had come to mean so much to Linda handed her a small box. Reaching inside, Linda found a beautiful blue Bible. Stenciled in gold letters on the front was her name, Linda Kay Davis.

With tears in her eyes, the girl clutched the Bible to her heart. It was the first Bible that she had ever had that was brand-new and all hers. Smiling, Mrs. Smith nodded her head and hugged her favorite pupil. Knowing that time was running out, Linda tried to find the words to tell the older woman just what she meant to her. Try as she might, they didn't come. As she said good-bye to Mrs. Smith for the last time, her heart ached because she simply couldn't say what she felt.

Linda couldn't look at the Bible without thinking of the woman who had been such a great role model for her. When she moved to Nashville, she took it with her. When she got married, it came along. When she went on the road for her first major concert tour, it was there. Yet more than the Bible, a part of Mrs. Smith was with her too. Mrs. Smith's love of the Lord, her sweet spirit, her positive attitude—they had all become a part of Linda's personality. Without realizing it, Linda was trying very hard to embrace the special elements of her mentor's life.

Almost a decade after high school, another woman came into the singer's life. Reba McEntire recognized the bright young woman's talents, and she too encouraged her to use them. She believed in Linda so much that she offered her the opportunity to join her company.

When Linda cut her first album, the famous redhead brought her a song that she had cowritten just a few months before. Knowing Linda's sweet nature, Reba felt that the song would be special to her. What she didn't know was that it would put into words something Linda herself had wanted to say for a long time.

When Linda recorded the song, she cried. Then, as she sang it for a show to be aired on national television, she cried again. No matter where she was, she couldn't sing it without thinking of Mrs. Smith. She had no idea where that special woman was living or what she was doing, but Linda desperately wanted her to know how much she had influenced her life. Still, there seemed to be no way.

A few months later, in El Dorado, Arkansas, a smiling woman named Marguerete Smith Miller turned on the television and sat down to watch a broadcast featuring a young woman she had once known. She was so proud. Linda had grown into a beautiful young woman, and the older woman could still see the sweet spirit in her eyes. One look told Mrs. Miller that this former Sunday school student of hers was still walking with the Lord; this one person made all the years of teaching Sunday school worthwhile. As the show went on, Mrs. Miller was deeply moved by the performance. There was one song in particular that seemed to have a special message, and she thought she detected tears in Linda's eyes as she sang it. Marguerete Smith Miller couldn't have known that she had caused the tears in Linda's big blue eyes. As she listened to the words, she couldn't help but be moved too.

You always know just what to do
You're someone I can look up to
I'd be a better me
If I could only be like you

There are many who believe that a mere Sunday school teacher has no impact on students, young or old. Many are predicting the end of the two-century-old Sunday school movement. But Linda Davis knows differently, as do the scores who were taught by Mrs. Smith. Thousands of Sunday school teachers have had an impact on millions of lives in one-on-one settings. Without them giving of their time and talents as teachers and role models, the world probably would never have known the likes of Dr. Billy Graham and scores of other Christian leaders.

"I wish I could be more like Mrs. Smith," Linda often tells groups, but one look into Linda's eyes reveals that she is not only a great deal like her, she has taken Mrs. Smith's positive influence to heart. Her Christian recording of "I Have Arrived" became the anthem embraced by actor Christopher Reeve in his battle with paralysis. Her constant work with charities has helped raise millions of dollars for the Muscular Dystrophy Association as well as for a number of other philanthropic endeavors all around the globe. Thanks to the caring, loving dedication of a junior high Sunday school teacher, Linda Davis—entertainer, inspirational speaker, mother, Christian leader, and church volunteer—has truly become "a better me." Why did all of this success and outreach happen? Because of the example of one Sunday school teacher who set a model for all other Sunday school teachers. Linda Davis, like millions of other adults whose morality was shaped in childhood at Sunday schools, is a living testimony of a woman who cared enough to get involved at church. If there were more Hannah Mores and Mrs. Smiths, then the Sunday school movement would still be the greatest tool in shaping the lives of future Christian leaders.

5

HARRIET TUBMAN

Faith to Lead

Born with four strikes against her, Harriet refused to give up in the face of overwhelming odds. She was the Moses of her time, who used her Christian faith as her compass and guide. No one stood as tall as did this tiny woman.

It was well past two in the morning and a fog was starting to blanket the ground as the short black woman resolutely strolled through the rural cemetery gates. Waiting for her, among hand-carved wooden grave markers, were about a dozen poorly dressed men and women. They had sneaked away from the plantations and farms where they worked, some running more than six miles through woods and across swamps, to see this tiny woman. Most of the twelve had never met each other. What bound them together on this cold winter night was the color of their skin, the fact that the state of Maryland considered each of them property, and a common desire to taste freedom before they died.

All those waiting in that cemetery had heard the name Harriet Tubman. She was a legend! At night in tiny cabins and during the day in the hot fields they had whispered of her exploits and marveled at the freedom runs she had made. To these slaves, Tubman was an almost mythological figure endowed with superhuman strength, courage, and cunning. They were each convinced there had never been a woman like her. They also believed that God had created Tubman for this special moment in time, and it was he who had blessed them with her leadership.

As Harriet approached the group, she sensed their fear and understood it. If captured, they would surely be beaten and then probably sold and taken south. There they would likely live in subhuman conditions as they were worked to death under an unforgiving sun. Harriet understood that risk better than most because she had once been one of them: a woman born into slavery, a woman beaten, a woman who had grown so tired of being a piece of property that she had finally made a mad dash she knew would either lead to freedom or death. She had been so driven by her passion to escape bondage that she hadn't stopped running until she reached Pennsylvania. That had been eight years ago in 1849, at a time when there was no Fugitive Slave Act, when just getting to the North meant freedom for every black man or woman who had the good fortune and stamina to make the perilous trip. Now things were much different. Even Harriet, who had lived as a free woman for eight years, could be arrested, placed in chains, and returned to those who had title to her body. To be truly free, a slave now had to reach Canada. Hence, what had once been a tough trail of ninety miles from the eastern shores of Maryland to Philadelphia was now a trek of hundreds of miles through rugged country until the journey finally ended in another nation.

Harriet looked deeply into the eyes of those with the courage to join her on this night. She saw them watch her as she approached and wondered if they were disappointed in what they saw. Tubman knew she did not physically measure up to the stories told about her exploits. Those who had come to follow her to freedom had surely expected a giant woman blessed with amazing strength. She was middle-aged, barely five feet tall, her skin dark as coal, her frame muscled but thin. She didn't look like a person who could outthink and outrun the United States government. But on more than a dozen occasions she had made this trip as a guide, and that is why there was now a $40,000 price on her head.

Those who had gathered on this night knew that just the mention of Harriet Tubman drove slave owners into a wild-eyed frenzy. Thousands of plantation owners and businessmen honestly feared she would lead the Southern slaves into outright rebellion. They felt she was more of a menace than John Brown and Frederick Douglass combined. Many would have personally paid the huge bounty to see her brought in either dead or alive. If they had known she was meeting in a cemetery on this night, a posse of hundreds would have been riding at top speed to apprehend the famous fugitive. Yet the word had not gotten out, so for the moment, Tubman was safe.

At this meeting, as she had at scores of others, Harriet introduced herself to the runaways by recalling a Bible story. It was a tale she had embraced since childhood. As the men and women drew closer, they were caught up by Tubman's raspy tone and obvious charisma even more than they were from her telling of a people bound in slavery in another time and in a distant place. They listened intently as the woman spoke of a man who seemed unsuited for leadership. She explained that this man lacked the skills necessary to inspire anyone to follow him, but nevertheless God chose him above all others. He was the Lord's man, she explained, and then she laughed as she added, and with God on his side, Moses performed great miracles that led his people out of slavery and to the Promised Land.

"The God of Moses is with you tonight," she assured them as she had many others. Then she added, her voice rising to the heavens, "He has sent me to guide you out of this Egypt and to our Promised Land. I have been there and it is a place where you can truly be free. Your life is your own in the North. If you have the faith, you can take the Underground Railroad all the way to freedom."

Harriet looked at the group for signs of doubt. The moment they had seen her face and observed the long, deep scar on her forehead, they possessed too much knowledge to ever go back to their past lives. There would be no turning back. Harriet realized that a slave who returned from one of these trips could betray too many secrets. As she studied their faces again, she leaned on a rifle she always carried with her on her trips to the South. The gun was her staff, her symbol of power, as well as a way to convince any whose courage failed them to continue to run for freedom.

After waiting a few moments for this new group of runners to consider the symbolism of the biblical story of Moses, Harriet spoke again, this time weaving a tale much closer to home. She told them about her days in slavery. She showed them the marks on her back, inflicted by a woman who had decided to teach the slave a lesson. She then revealed how she had been beaten so badly as a child she almost died from injuries. She pointed to the scar she still carried on her forehead as a testament to that beating.

Harriet explained to the listeners that she had taken the blow to the head in order to protect another slave. When an overseer had picked up a two-pound weight and was going to use it to beat his "property" into submission, the tiny woman had stepped between them. In rage at her lack of propriety, the overseer had taken the hunk of iron and struck Harriet so hard that it created a deep indentation in her forehead. As her skull cracked, she fell to the ground, blood freely flowing from the wound. She almost died that night, and it would take over a year before Harriet could begin to live a normal life. Yet she now felt that that day was just a test: God wanted to see if she had the faith to offer her life to save one of her own people.

Harriet Tubman then revealed that even in those times when she hovered in great pain between life and death, God was with her. She told of an experience she attributed as a gift from her Lord. "When I was almost dead, I flew. I flew above the earth and looked down on the land as a bird in flight."

The runners had heard about such experiences in biblical stories, but the realization that a member of their race had been so touched by God gave them a new sense of faith. Each understood that the Lord gave this woman her courage, vision, and strength, and that she would freely lay down her life for them just as she had risked her life so many years before as a child. They were assured that God came for all people, not just for those who claimed to be their owners.

In the twenty-five years since she had been struck in the head, Harriet had been plagued by tremendous headaches. Some were so strong they caused her to black out. Those who gathered around her during these attacks often believed she was dying. It was during these episodes when the visions continued and grew more detailed. She was always flying, but now with a purpose and a goal. She would awaken refreshed with the knowledge the Lord was showing her the path to freedom.

The visions expanded her faith and gave her courage. Initially she could not convince even family members that God had a plan for her life, and that plan included escaping to the North. Finally, at the age of twenty-eight, when she was told she was about to be sold to a new master, she prayed a short prayer and stole away in the middle of the night.

Those listening to her in the graveyard leaned forward as the woman whispered, "Like Moses, I turned my face toward the north, fixed my eyes on the guiding star, and committed my way unto the Lord to lead me on this long journey."

At that time Harriet knew nothing about the Underground Railroad and had no idea who to contact to help her on her way, but she honestly felt the Lord's hand guiding her every step. It was as if she had already seen each fork in the road, each river, and each hill. Even though she had never taken this path before, she knew the way. While working in a field one day, Harriet Tubman had been befriended by a local white woman. She sensed that God had sent this woman to her for a purpose. So a few hours after she started her run to freedom and trusting in her faith, Harriet stopped by that woman's home. That "angel" gave her a piece of paper and directions to a safe house. The next contact guided her to another. And over the course of several days the runaway slave was able to make the trip to Pennsylvania.

Those gathered that night in the cemetery marveled as Harriet told of her dash for freedom. They listened intently as she explained how the Underground Railroad worked and how every person who was part of the system was risking their life so that each of them could taste freedom. Only after she had told them about the friends they had waiting to help them did she finally describe to them the real motivation for risking their lives on this trip.

"When I walked into Pennsylvania, I looked at my hands to see if I was the same person, now that I was free. There was such a glory over everything. The sun came like gold through the trees, and over the fields, and I felt like I was in heaven."

Heaven on earth, she assured them, was waiting for each of them. She reiterated that she had been sent to set her people free. Then, as if to guarantee that they would soon experience what she had, she added, "I have been doing this for years. More than three hundred have ridden the train with me, and I never run my train off the track, and I never lost a single passenger."

As the men and women thought about what lay in front of them, Harriet began to sing "Go Down Moses." One by one, each of the runaways joined her. Soon, across the graveyard and into the forest, a chorus shouted out to God that they were ready to trust him just as his people had thousands of years before. They were ready to follow this fugitive slave to freedom.

In the 1850s, Harriet Tubman was called the "Moses of American slaves." Gaining her freedom had not been enough to satisfy her soul; she was driven to bring that freedom to as many as she could. This drive to bring freedom would be the defining thread that continued through the rest of her life. Thus, when it was unsafe for any man or woman of color to travel alone across the Mason-Dixon Line, this ex-slave went back to the South time and time again to lead others through the American wilderness to freedom. She wore her shoes out on these trips, often coming within seconds of death, but she would not quit. She felt this was why she had been put on this earth, why her mother had taught her Bible stories, and why she had been put through so many trials as a slave. It was all to prepare for this task. In the churches and abolitionist meetings where she spoke to raise awareness and funds for her mission, she explained she had been called by God to set her people free.

"I had reasoned this out in my mind," she would tell those who gathered to hear her. "There was one of two things I had a right to, liberty or death; if I could not have one, I would have the other. For no man should take me alive. I should fight for my liberty as long as my strength lasted, and when the time came for me to go, the Lord would let them take me."

Within a month of gaining her freedom, Harriet began working long hours as a cook and maid, saving every penny to help pay for the freedom runs of others. So great was her passion and so powerful her obvious and outspoken convictions that only a few months after she arrived in Philadelphia she was made an official "conductor" on the Underground Railroad. Harriet was so deeply trusted by powerful white abolitionists, she was one of the few, black or white, who knew all the routes and contacts on this secret freedom road. Even with the tempting price put on her head and the fact that the 1850 Fugitive Slave Act made it illegal for any citizen to assist an escaped slave, she continued for another decade to make dangerous treks into slave states to organize her freedom marches. Nothing, not even threats on her life, could dissuade this woman from what she called "the Lord's work."

By 1857, Harriet Tubman was so respected that she was invited to join a circle of very famous and influential Americans, including Susan B. Anthony, William H. Seward, Ralph Waldo Emerson, Horace Mann, and Louisa May Alcott. Soon Harriet, who could neither read nor write, became one of the most recognized speakers in the antislavery movement. She was so important to this cause that her friends begged her to allow others to guide runaway slaves to freedom. But she refused to stay in the safety of the North, explaining she could not give up her work any more than Moses could give up leading the children of Israel. Besides, she assured them, since she had been called to this work by the Lord, God would protect her on her missions.

When the first shots were fired at Fort Sumter, it seemed as though Harriet's heroic actions were no longer needed. Surely, most believed, her job was done. But the Civil War prompted the deeply religious woman to seek a new direction for her faith.

Her visions now had her flying above battlegrounds. She felt those dreams were a sign she needed to be involved in serving those fighting for the freedom of millions of slaves. Initially she volunteered as a nurse, bandaging the wounds of both white and black soldiers. She prayed with men as they fought back the pain, held them as doctors amputated injured limbs, and sang spirituals as they sought to reach some understanding of their suffering. And she always thanked them for all her people. Tubman treated thousands during the first months of the Civil War and would have gladly continued her nursing care if her government had not assigned her to a duty believed to be even more important.

In 1862, Harriet Tubman was assigned as a nurse and teacher to the Gullah people of the Sea Islands, off the coast of South Carolina. When she set up programs for these ex-slaves, Harriet was given the task of going into the South as a spy. Like Joshua, she went undercover and found weak points in the enemy's lines. Her understanding of war strategy proved to be so remarkable that the uneducated ex-slave was actually put in charge of African-American troops assigned to disrupt Southern supply lines. She led several raids that destroyed bridges and railroads.

After watching Harriet direct her military strikes, General Rufus Saxton wrote to Secretary of War Edwin Stanton trying to explain her vital service to the Union. In his letter, the Union general described what he had witnessed as an important American first. "This is the only military command in American history wherein a woman, black or white, led the raid and under whose inspiration it was originated and conducted."

Press coverage of her exploits made Harriet an even larger hero in the Civil War than she had been in the days leading up to it. She proved, as both a woman and an African American, that she was worthy of being treated as an equal member of American society. She would soon find this was not to be the case. When the war ended, Harriet was a legend throughout the country, yet she was paid only $200 for her four years of service to her nation.

Settling into life as a truly free woman, she felt lost. She needed a cause. She didn't feel that God had placed her on earth to tarry. She looked for new ways to serve.

Because she had never attended school, Harriet knew the limitations placed upon those who could neither read nor write. Returning to the South, she watched as illiterate free men and women struggled to do even the most elementary of tasks. She knew that without knowledge, freedom was only a word. To thrive, former slaves would have to learn basic educational skills. She set about establishing schools for freed slaves in South Carolina. She found empty buildings, secured funds, and recruited teachers. Through her hard work, thousands were given the tools she had been denied. For many ex-slaves, this education would be the first step toward gaining a true sense of self-worth and independence.

As Harriet spoke to groups in an attempt to raise awareness of the need to educate ex-slaves and their children, she discovered another flaw in the American system. She could not vote. Joining with women like Susan B. Anthony, Harriet Tubman asked the nation's leaders to expand freedom for all through the vote. She preached the need for a new kind of train, a train that would lead to full representation and the vote for women and minorities. At every stop she taught that blacks and women had to gain the vote to become full partners in the American experience, that the vote would lead to a new type of freedom for the unrepresented and the oppressed. While she put some of the first rails down for this dream, it would be those she inspired who would finish the job on this railroad of ideas and truth.

Even as she was honored in front of large forums and lionized for being the Moses to her people, Harriet felt she was not fully using her faith. She sensed she had a deeper calling, one not found in the Old Testament, but in the words of Jesus. She prayed for a way to expand her Christian work.

In the days after the war, Harriet Tubman noted that everywhere she traveled, the very young and the very old struggled to get by. There were children living on the streets and elderly men and women on corners begging for scraps of food. The homeless were everywhere. Worst of all, it seemed the government and many of the churches did not feel any compassion for the masses of poor people struggling just to find a meal or a place to sleep.

Moving to Auburn, New York, Harriet married a man she had cared for as a nurse in the war and discovered a way to embrace the message of Christ. Almost immediately after their marriage, Harriet and Nelson Davis welcomed several young orphans into their home. They raised these waifs as if they were their own. Soon a pregnant blind woman and her four children joined them. Then came a crush of older former slaves who were homeless. Tubman worked day and night just to feed her growing brood. To make ends meet, she raised chickens, pigs, and cows and tended a huge garden. She worked as a maid, took in laundry, and worked any odd jobs she could find. When her friends asked why she was doing so much for those who could pay her nothing, she simply asked them to read Matthew 25:35–40. In Harriet's mind, each needy person represented Christ. She therefore could not turn anyone away from her door, no matter their age or color. It was her job to free the poor from the slavery of poverty, handicap, and age.

To finance her support of others, Harriet worked with a teacher, Sarah Hopkins Bradford, and published *Scenes in the Life of Harriet Tubman*. This book enhanced the legend of Harriet Tubman and sent her story around the globe. Queen Victoria was so taken by the faith of the ex-slave, she invited Harriet to Great Britain and asked her to stay in the palace. When Harriet was unable to make the trip, the queen sent her a silver medal that decreed the debt even the people of England felt they owed this remarkable woman.

Though now an international hero, Harriet barely scraped by. Every dollar she earned was quickly given away to those she felt needed it more than she did. As the years went by and she continued to live for "the least of these," the American "Moses" assumed she would be forgotten. Thirty years after the war, Harriet labored alone, far out of the spotlight, while a new group was being founded to carry on her vision of freedom.

In 1896, the National Association of Colored Women held its first convention. And this new generation of African-American women asked Harriet Tubman to be their keynote speaker. At seventy-five, Harriet stood at the podium and gazed out at faces she did not recognize. As she studied this new band of energetic leaders preparing to fight for new freedoms, she was reminded of her clandestine late-night graveyard meetings with men and women who simply wanted a chance to be free. So much had changed in four decades. Harriet marveled at how she was now able to share her message in the open, to speak freely in addressing women of color, many of whom had never known what it was like to be considered a piece of property.

She cleared her throat and began to speak. Harriet told the women that she was no longer the Moses who needed to lead slaves to freedom. Her calling now was to help those who once were slaves to escape poverty in their old age. This poverty, she said, was holding these people in chains just like slavery once had. She asked for this new generation to reach out to these men and women who had given so much and received so little. After thunderous applause, Harriet Tubman stepped down from the platform and stepped out of the national spotlight.

Returning to Auburn, she set about trying to live the words she had spoken to the NACW. She took what little money she had and the property she owned and established a home for aged former slaves. In 1911, she herself moved into that home. Two years later, at the age of ninety-one, she asked for her friends and family to gather. She had lived her life for others. She had spent years leading slaves to freedom and, as a free woman, reaching out to the least of these enslaved by poverty. During those years Harriet had not just spoken about her faith; she had lived it. And even though she was now as poor as she had been as a slave, she felt like a queen. After all, unlike Moses, she had not just led her children to the Promised Land, she had walked on that land, built a home there, and gotten to taste a bit of the milk and honey.

Now, as Harriet felt death approaching, she had one final vision to share with her loved ones. This vision was of a freedom that was not of this earth. So as those who had followed her for so many years gathered by her bedside, she whispered, "I go away to prepare a place for you, that where I am you also may be." A few minutes later, the ex-slave boarded the glory train as a truly free woman.

Harriet Tubman, a woman born a slave, was buried with full military honors, including a flag-draped coffin. Since her death she has been memorialized in scores of ways, including the naming of a liberty ship after her, in 1944, and a commemorative postage stamp bearing her name and likeness issued in 1996. Yet she is remembered today mostly because she used her faith and God's gift to respond to a call that took her from being one of "the least of these" to impacting the lives of millions who truly were "the least of these." She may have been the American Moses, but Harriet Tubman lived her life by embracing Matthew 25:35–40.

6

FANNY CROSBY

Faith to Exceed Expectations

She seemed born to write, but the woman who gave the world some of its most inspiring hymns had to fight two kinds of darkness before seeing the light. Fanny's story is one of more than words and music, it's all about searching for a purpose while overcoming doubts and fears.

In 1905, the promise inscribed on the Statue of Liberty rang hollow for many. For most new immigrants life was tough, living conditions were often horrid, and the promise of opportunity was as illusive as the gold at the end of the rainbow.

On a blustery late winter day in Manhattan, a tiny, frail, stooped, and seemingly forgotten old woman walked the streets near the rough-and-tumble Bowery district. Her bonnet, dress, and shoes were something a stylish woman of 1840 would have worn, but were completely out of place that day on the Big Apple's crowded streets.

If her clothes did not give away the fact she was struggling to get by, her home did. The woman lived in a rooming house with a dozen other families, most of whom could not speak English. Her tiny room was barely large enough for a bed and desk. There was no window for ventilation, so it was always dark, damp, and dusty. Yet the frail woman did not care that her residence was shoddy, that her neighbors spoke different languages, or that the streets were filled with rowdy kids, shipyard workers, drunks, prostitutes, and gamblers. In fact, she seemed to relish her association with these struggling masses.

This poor old woman did not walk the streets alone, though it was not for security reasons. She took her strolls with a companion because she was blind. To her the world was a place of dark, shapeless shadows. But she didn't fear the endless void that stretched out before her; in fact she took comfort in the darkness.

On this March day, as the elderly woman made her way down the congested sidewalks, few took the time to greet her. Those who did were not members of society, but the rejects of the Bowery, men and women who drank away their troubles and fought in the streets to settle debts. These castoffs spoke to the tiny woman in gushing tones filled with respect and admiration. She smiled and replied with a word of encouragement. She often reached into her purse to hand someone a coin.

Even though just a decade and a half short of being a century old, this woman's stride indicated she was on a mission. She was headed to one of her favorite places, a local prison. And though none of the men living behind iron bars were any relation to her, she considered them to be a part of her family. When everyone else had written them off, this woman took the time to show them their potential and to assure each of these brothers that God loved them and that forgiveness was just a prayer away.

As she continued along streets crowded with streetcars, automobiles, and horse-drawn carts, no one could have guessed she had addressed Congress on three different occasions, once when she was just a teen. Who would have believed this old bent woman had penned a best-selling book while still in her twenties and composed more than eight thousand songs. And who could have known, as she made her way merrily along the Brooklyn sidewalks, that churches all over the world were about to set aside an entire Sunday to honor the blind woman's contributions to the Christian faith. But that is exactly what was going to happen on March 26, 1905. Congregations all over America, Europe, Asia, and Africa were going to fill the air with the songs of the woman called "The Methodist Saint."

So how did the world's greatest gospel music composer, a woman whose hymns are still sung by hundreds of millions, end up residing among some of the world's greatest sinners? It was a matter of prayer, faith, hard work, and a dramatic midlife change of direction, and it would never have been possible without the input of four very different, but very special, people.

Fanny Crosby is probably the most unlikely of all American success stories. Born in 1820 in rural New York State, she started with two huge strikes against her. At the age of six weeks, an inept doctor improperly treated an eye infection, causing blindness. A few months later, Fanny's father, the family's breadwinner, suddenly died. What was before her mother, twenty-one-year-old Mercy Crosby, seemed a task too large for any woman, but on faith she pushed ahead. Hiring out as a maid, she toiled long hours to make barely enough to keep a roof over her girl's head.

The blind child, Frances Jane, should have been pushed aside, forgotten, tended to but not taught; that was the usual way during that period. Handicapped people were shunned or ignored, kept out of site, often viewed as a punishment from God. Yet Fanny had been blessed. Her grandmother, Eunice, refused to view the child as anything but a gift and was determined that the tiny girl would be given every opportunity to grow, to explore, and to secure the tools to succeed.

Rather than keep Fanny shut up inside the family's small home, Eunice opened the door and let the child explore the world. She allowed her to fall down, then urged her to get back up. She gave Fanny a sense of worth by praising her for accomplishing even the most menial of tasks. Most importantly, Eunice taught her to see by touching and listening. Thus the child developed keen senses few could begin to fathom. And, even though it was unheard of during the period, Eunice had Fanny mainstreamed in school.

Though her teachers in the multigrade one-room schoolhouses had no time for individual instruction, they could not help but note the way Fanny soaked in all they taught. She was like a sponge, remembering every detail of a lesson, and she was able to recite almost verbatim lessons in rhetoric and literature. In her third year of school, Fanny discovered poetry. The way the lines flowed awakened the child's mind to a beauty others were unable to see. To her the words were alive and took Fanny to places others could not imagine. Her fascination with rhythm and rhyme became almost a compulsion. For hours the eight-year-old would play with words, reshaping them into patterns that gave her life substance and depth. In a world where most were unsure of how to deal with the blind child, poetry became her vehicle of understanding.

Oh, what a happy child I am, although I cannot see!
I am resolved that in this world contented I will be!
How many blessings I enjoy that other people don't!
So weep or sigh because I'm blind, I cannot—nor I won't.

At church, at school, and in the local shops, those who met Fanny were amazed by her abilities, but they also realized that in rural New York, her lack of vision would doom her to be little more than a novelty. So while this endearing, happy child brought many great joys, she also haunted them. Soon the community came together in an attempt to do something for the Crosby girl.

Pooling their money, the Crosby family's friends sent Mercy and her daughter to New York City to meet with the world's foremost eye specialist, Dr. Valentine Mott. Mott examined the girl and shook his head. Sadness filled his voice as he whispered to Fanny, "Poor child, I am afraid you will never see again."

The physician was amazed by the tiny girl's response. She didn't cry; rather, as she heard the news, a smile crept across her face. She assured Mott and her mother that she was fine, that no one should pity her, and though her eyes could not perceive as others did, she could still see with her heart.

More determined than ever that her granddaughter's intellectual curiosity was fully challenged, Eunice began to read the works of two blind poets, Homer and Milton. Being able to hear the words of those who suffered as she did inspired Fanny to compose more verses. Thanks again to her grandmother, she was able to share her poems at church and at community gatherings. While many marveled at her God-given abilities, most believed Fanny's remarkable talents were wasted on someone who could not see.

While still going to school, Fanny began to realize she was falling behind her classmates. Not being able to read or write was stunting her intellectual growth and leaving her thirsting for the knowledge she could not access because she could not see.

Eunice sensed her granddaughter's frustration and redoubled her efforts to expose her to the world. They went for walks in the woods. The older woman would have Fanny hold a leaf while she would describe it in detail. She kept repeating this hands-on experience, having Fanny touch everything from rocks to animals, from streams to trees. Whatever the two came across, Eunice would literally paint exhaustingly detailed verbal pictures of each new experience. Yet the grandmother soon sensed it was not enough.

More and more her lack of sight was shutting Fanny off from the world. Fanny was able to do fewer and fewer things at school. The games her friends were playing could no longer be adapted to meet her special needs. In a world that seemed to be expanding daily for most children, Fanny felt the walls closing in on her. Wise beyond her years, she realized that the wonders of life were forever going to be just out of reach. While she had learned a great deal more than most blind children of the period, she fully realized she would never be able to read, write, or live independently. She had hit a wall and there was no way over it and no path around it.

One summer evening, while the two sat in a rocking chair, eleven-year-old Fanny asked Eunice a troubling question, "Does God hear my prayers?"

"Yes," came the woman's immediate reply.

Falling to her knees, Eunice at her side, the normally long-winded Fanny put forth a simple petition, "Dear Lord, please show me how I can learn like other children." It was a prayer she would repeat over and over again for the next three years.

It was with tears in her eyes that Eunice Crosby put her granddaughter to bed that night. The child's prayer had broken her heart. The steady, sure Calvinist woman wanted to believe that God had a purpose for her sightless granddaughter. But now, as she considered how confining Fanny's world would always be, even Eunice was at a loss to know what that purpose could be.

A few months later, Eunice suddenly grew ill. She was just fifty-three, but hard work and disease had left her old beyond her years. Eunice's voice, once steady and expressive, was weak and unsure.

As she sensed the end was coming, Eunice called out for her granddaughter. Mercy brought the little girl to her grandmother's bedside. In a soft voice Eunice turned toward the child, rested her hand on the girl's face, and made what seemed to those gathered around the bed a very unusual request. "Fanny, tell me, will you meet your grandma in our Father's house on high?"

Fanny swallowed deeply, choking back tears, and replied, "By the grace of God I will."

Eunice wrapped her arms around her granddaughter, hugged her a final time, and then eased back into the bed. Within hours she was gone.

Fanny's grandmother had been her teacher, her strongest supporter, and her best friend, as well as her eyes. Without Eunice, Fanny's world shrank. Other local women, including the family's landlord, tried to fill the gap, but they could not. Even when her mother remarried and two sisters were added to her life, Fanny still felt shut off from much of the real world. There were places she could go, friends she could visit, household chores she could do, but there was no one to paint vivid pictures of all the things she could not see.

On an early November day, Fanny opted to visit the local school and listen to the other children do their lessons. As she returned home, her keen hearing noted her mother's footsteps rushing up to meet her. She also heard the rustling of paper. As Fanny would later explain, "I thought it was a letter and someone must be sick or have died." Yet this time her instincts were wrong. Mercy had been sent news of a school for the blind in New York City. After she explained to her daughter what this might mean, Fanny shouted, "Oh, thank God, he has answered my prayer, just as I knew he would."

The Institution for the Blind offered Fanny a chance to grow as she never had. She was taught to read with her fingers, to write, to listen carefully to teachers, and she was challenged to think. And, when she revealed her talent in composing poetry, Fanny was pushed to expand her knowledge by listening to the work of revered masters, such as Milton, and then translate what she learned into her own words.

The Institution for the Blind was an early beacon of education in America. What was taking place behind the walls on Ninth Street was so revolutionary that some of the nation's most respected men and women often stopped by the school and observed the students. The great William Cullen Bryant visited and, after hearing Fanny recite some of her poetry, told the teenager how impressed he was. Encouraged, Fanny continued to create, and as her work improved, the school allowed her to compose special poems for each of the school's guests. Fanny soon came to know John Quincy Adams, Martin Van Buren, William Henry Harrison, John Tyler, and James Polk. Few Americans of the period had ever met even one president, but by the time she was eighteen, the small blind girl counted all the living former first executives as well as the current national leader as her mentors and friends. In fact, these great men were so moved by her poetry they asked her to address Congress in hopes she would inspire more funding for schools for the blind all across America.

By the time she was twenty, Fanny's poems became a regular feature in several New York City newspapers and periodicals. Her published works embraced a myriad of subjects, including history, politics, personalities, love, and nature. She was intent on her writing becoming a path to fame and fortune.

In 1844, with the national release of her book *The Blind Girl and Other Poems*, Fanny took a huge step toward achieving her goal. She followed that success by joining with famed bandleader George Root to compose the first cantata published in America. Although her name became known throughout New England, she was not making enough money to leave the institute, so Fanny became an instructor at the school. She would hold that position for the next thirteen years.

One of the other teachers, a devout Christian she knew only as Mr. Jones, was deeply impressed with her work, but concerned about her attitude. He saw no spiritual depth in anything Fanny produced. After watching her bask in the glory of adoration freely given by another round of important guests, he approached Fanny and gave her a stern warning, "Remember that whatever talent you possess belongs wholly to God and that you ought to give him the credit for all you do."

A seed had been planted, but it would be many years before the teacher's words would take root. It wasn't until Fanny was faced with the greatest tragedy of her life that she recalled what Jones had said.

In 1851, a cholera epidemic swept New York City. People who experienced the wave of illness claimed death could be smelled in every corner of the city. Fanny could sense the uncertainty that hovered around her. She heard the horror stories of those who had suddenly grown sick and died, and for the first time she considered her own mortality. The frequent news of death caused her to remember the death of her grandmother and the promise she had made. Fanny wondered if she truly was a Christian. This haunting question drove her from her room at the institute and into the streets. Her trip ended at John Street Methodist Church, where a revival was in progress. For three nights she attended the services, going forward at every altar call, but she felt no change.

On the third night, as the choir began to sing an old Isaac Watts hymn, her despair began to lift. When the singers reached the third line of the fifth stanza of "Alas Did My Savior Bleed," the blind woman stood up and shouted, "Here, Lord, I give myself away!" It was as if she could finally see!

For those who know Crosby's work, it would seem this conversion experience would have immediately plunged her into composing Christian prose. It did not. Over the next few years many of her poems were published, in individual and book form, and all of them remained secular in nature. While convinced she was saved, Fanny remained intent on using her talents to achieve secular fame and fortune. In fact, she was still so unsure of her faith that she would not even pray in public.

On March 5, 1858, at the age of thirty-seven, Fanny married a former student and teacher at the institute, Alexander Van Alstyne. Not long after she married, Fanny discovered she was pregnant. She could not wait to bring a new life into the world. Each night she prayed her child would be given the gift of sight along with her own uniquely developed sense of observation. Yet soon after her child was born, it died. Fanny was crushed. The only way she could deal with the loss was to pick up her pen and put her emotions onto paper. What resulted was the first hymn she would ever write, "Safe in the Arms of Jesus."

Jesus, my heart's dear Refuge,
Jesus has died for me;
Firm on the Rock of Ages
Ever my trust shall be.
Here let me wait with patience,
Wait till the night is o'er;
Wait till I see the morning
Break on the golden shore

Except for the words in that song, Fanny Crosby would never speak of the loss of her child. She buried that emotional story along with the baby. As Dutch Reformed minister Peter Stryker listened to "Safe in the Arms of Jesus," he sensed that with the death of the baby had been born a unique vision. He studied "Safe in the Arms of Jesus" and noted a personal depth and message that he felt mirrored what those in his congregation needed to hear.

Stryker convinced Fanny to meet with one of his close friends, William Bradbury. A well-known Christian composer and publisher, Bradbury was looking for a poet to supply his firm with dynamic Christian verse. The publisher was tired of stilted and formal prose. He wanted to present personal words that could touch hearts and reach souls. After one meeting with the tiny woman, Bradbury realized Fanny's gift was the answer to his prayers.

Beginning at the age of forty-four, Fanny would pen three to five new gospel songs a week. The more she wrote, the more consumed she was with a zeal to live each word, each verse, each chorus. By the time she was fifty, she was America's most popular gospel music writer. The evangelistic team of Dwight L. Moody and Ira D. Sankey took Fanny's songs to every corner of the world. One reporter noted, "Johann Strauss reigned in Vienna as the 'Waltz King,' and John Phillip Sousa in Washington as the 'March King,' but Fanny Crosby reigned all over the world as the 'Hymn Queen.'"

At an age when most women were seeking a quiet life, Fanny, who once would not pray in front of others, was speaking at America's largest churches, traveling to every corner of America, spreading the story of her faith and providing inspiration to all who suffered from handicaps. Hundreds, such as Helen Keller, seized upon this tiny woman as a role model, and many of her legion of fans broke down barriers in education, industry, and society.

By the time Fanny Crosby Day was celebrated in March 1905, the songwriter was eighty-five years old and had penned more than seven thousand hymns. The prayers of her youth had been answered: she finally had great fame and the opportunity for a small fortune. Yet she turned her back on the latter. Spending only the barest amount on herself, the tiny woman gave the rest to those she considered "the least of these." She continued to walk the slum streets because she felt that is where the Lord's Word needed to be heard and where a Christian example of love needed to be felt.

"It seemed intended by the blessed providence of God," she would tell each audience, "that I should be blind all my life, and I thank him for the dispensation. If perfect earthly sight were offered me tomorrow, I would not accept it. I might not have sung hymns to the praise of God if I had been distracted by the beautiful and interesting things about me. If I had a choice, I would still choose to remain blind ... for when I die, the first face I will ever see will be the face of my blessed Savior."

The blind poet would live another ten years after the day that honored her work worldwide. Even as her health failed and she was forced to live with caretakers, she continued to write and speak as well as share her love of the Lord with everyone she met. And when the end came, she was ready, by the grace of God, to see her grandmother in her Father's house.

It has been said that Fanny Crosby's songs have led more people to salvation than all the sermons of the greatest preachers and evangelists. Yet without a grandmother who would not allow the girl's potential to be lost, a teacher who constantly reminded Fanny her talents were on loan from God, a preacher who sensed her gifts could bring God's mission into great focus, and a famous hymn composer who gave her an opportunity to present her vision of the Lord to the world, no one would now remember the little blind girl from upstate New York or have ever been inspired by "Blessed Assurance," "All the Way My Savior Leads Me," "To God Be the Glory," "Pass Me Not, O Gentle Savior," "Safe in the Arms of Jesus," "Rescue the Perishing," "Jesus, Keep Me Near the Cross," "I Am Thine, O Lord," "Redeemed," and so many other incredible gospel classics.

7

LAURIE PRANGE

Faith in a Faithless World

One of Hollywood's most talented character actresses was tempted by a life that offered quick, shallow fixes. Thanks to the foundation of faith laid by her parents and the example of a woman who died long before she was born, Laurie became a light in a world where darkness often rules.

In a few moments Laurie Prange would walk the boards of the Los Angeles Art Theater as Blanche DuBois. Years before, Tennessee Williams had watched her perform in *Juno and the Paycock* at the Mark Tabor Forum. After the show, the award-winning playwright complimented her performance and suggested someday she play Laura in *The Glass Menagerie*. Now, after more than two decades of success in television and film, Laurie was starring in another of the Pulitzer Prize–winning writer's plays, *A Streetcar Named Desire*. She had barely been out of her teens when Williams had first approached her and probably was unprepared for the challenge the role offered. But now, with so many different roles behind her, she felt as if she was ready to follow in the footsteps of Oscar- and Tony-winning legends. These other women may have essayed this role, but Laurie was sure she had the ability to put her own spin on Blanche DuBois.

As the lights were adjusted and the audience spoke in hushed tones on the other side of the curtain, Laurie was strangely reminded of her mother. As if a time portal had opened up in front of her, she was again a child, a spectator hovering over her own Southern California home, watching as Evelyn Prange paused for prayer. That is the way her mother had always done things; when she faced challenges, she prayed. Laurie saw the scene as clearly as she had witnessed it countless times as a child. Evelyn, her light green eyes closed, an almost childlike expression on her face, softly said, "Now I lay me down to sleep. I pray the Lord my soul to keep." From there the gentle woman would always continue, remembering her friends and family, laying out all her problems and blessings, and concluding her petition with a heartfelt thank-you for God's guidance and love. When standing in prayer, Evelyn always seemed confident that nothing could stop her. Through her example, the mother passed along the power of prayer to her daughter.

Now, in the moments before the opening night of *Streetcar*, Laurie embraced her mother's practice, quietly bowing her head to seek the strength she needed to bring her God-given talents to life. Closing her eyes, just like her mother did before her, the actress silently opened a direct line to her Lord. Before her lips had moved or she had even finished contemplating her initial thought, she sensed someone by her side. Looking up, she noted a cast member.

"Are you praying?" the woman asked.

"Yes," Laurie answered.

"May I pray with you?" came the simple request.

"Certainly."

As the two joined hands and bowed their heads, a couple of the cast members approached. They didn't ask if they could become a part of this prayer circle; they simply bowed their heads and listened. Over the next few days, the cast, now joined by the crew, moved closer before each performance. Within a few weeks her prayer time included almost everyone involved with the production. One simple act, meant to go unnoticed, had opened the door for scores to come to God and ask for prayer. At first this universal response for spiritual guidance surprised the veteran actress, but when she considered how her parents' own quiet witness had impacted her life, she suddenly understood the full power of even the smallest act of faith. She also realized she had become the answer to her parents' prayers. It had taken a while and it had been a long road with many detours, but she was the Christian daughter they had petitioned God to place in their family. Laurie was carrying on the walk of faith that had brought the Pranges through the best and worst of times.

Before Laurie worked with the likes of James Arness, Robert Stack, Bette Davis, and a host of other entertainment superstars, she was simply the daughter of Joseph and Evelyn Prange of Culver City, California. She was just another kid who was fortunate enough to grow up in a tight-knit, loving family.

"I was raised in a Christian home with wonderful parents," Laurie explained. Her father, an Army Air Corps flyer during World War II, worked for Douglas Aircraft. It took all that he made to raise six children in a very modest two-bedroom home.

Joseph and Evelyn always put their children's happiness ahead of their own. They scrimped and saved to assure that the Prange kids were able to attend a private Lutheran school. But it was the couple's physical sacrifices that really set them apart.

"My parents allowed our home and backyard to be the center playground for the neighborhood," Laurie recalled, a smile etching her face. "We took over the house and the yard with four-story tree houses, huge forts, and even five-foot-deep tunnels behind the garage. Essentially my parents sacrificed tidy landscaping and 'order' in our house to have their kids nearby. All of the other kids in the neighborhood wanted to play at our house."

Evelyn Prange was a positive woman who believed in giving kindly advice rather than sharp scoldings. That gentleness, coupled with her giving nature, made her naturally approachable. Laurie was never afraid to talk about her problems with her mother. Even more remarkable, the neighborhood kids shared their dilemmas with the tiny woman too. Evelyn considered making lemonade and cookies and listening to kids as a witness and calling. Giving up time with her own friends did not bother her a bit. Most important, she encouraged kids to be themselves and told them how much "God-given" potential they had. After a few minutes with Evelyn, everyone seemed to believe they could live all their dreams. She held a strong influence over scores of kids, many of whom came from dysfunctional homes. Even these misfits were welcomed into the Prange home.

"My parents believed in sacrifice, in living Christian values each day of their lives, in fully accepting others, and, most of all, in forgiveness." Even as a child Laurie knew that, even in Christians, these were often principles that were hard to find. Yet they were always there in abundance at the Prange residence.

Growing up, Laurie saw her parents' sacrifice, acceptance, and forgiveness at church and at home. These principles showed strongly in everything from her father's business dealings to the way he offered grace at the dinner table. Essentially all Evelyn and Joseph asked of their children was that they live their faith in every facet of their lives. The parents assured their children that if they did, nothing could ever harm them.

Laurie saw these principles develop in not just her brothers and sisters but in the kids who made the Prange home the area playground. Laurie saw her parents make a lasting impact on these kids that was so strong, many took these lessons with them, applying them throughout their lives. The person who seemed to most embrace this giving heart was Laurie's oldest brother.

"When he went to college he would make trips to Mexico," Laurie recalled, "where he would help build homes for poor families. He was always reaching out to those around him who were in need. From an early age, when others were being selfish and putting themselves first, he was not."

Due to his giving nature and strong sense of right and wrong, Joey was someone Laurie wanted to emulate. She admired his convictions and was drawn to his desire to live a life that put others first.

"He felt so deeply about the value of each life," Laurie explained, "that when he was drafted he told us that although he would do his best to stay safe, he did not believe he could raise a gun to harm another man."

Even though he considered going to Canada, Joey did not run from the draft. As a Prange he had been raised to not turn one's back in fear and to accept responsibility as a part of life. When the time came, he went through boot camp and accepted his assignment in Vietnam. Still, the moral contradictions that raged in his soul made him question the justification of using a weapon for its intended purpose. His letters home reflected the conflict in his soul.

"I will never forget my father picking us up from Sunday school one morning," Laurie recalled. "All the way home he was looking straight ahead and saying nothing. Finally he asked us, 'Do you believe that God loves us and knows what is best for us and it is his will when we are to pass on?' I could not figure out why he was asking us this question. After all, we all believed in the power of faith. My sister was the first to see through his question. She sensed what had happened and demanded to know why Dad was asking us all this. In a trembling voice my father told us that Jesus had taken our brother Joey to be with him in heaven."

As if a dam had burst, unrelenting tears flooded Laurie's eyes. She had lost her hero, her role model, the person who probably most believed in the true nature of the living God's gentle and forgiving love, and she had lost him to a war he did not want to fight. Cries of grief filled the car as the family drove home.

"When friends and family members came to offer their support that Sunday afternoon," Laurie explained as she relived that horrible day, "I would not come out of the bedroom to greet them. That night I prayed I would wake up the next morning to this having been a bad dream, but instead I woke up to the sounds of my father's uncontrollable sobbing and realized that my wonderful, inspiring, dynamic, and loving brother really was gone. He would never be coming home from Vietnam. I would never talk with him or spend time with him again."

That day in 1967 turned Laurie's world upside down. The innocent bliss of life had been forever shattered. Seeking an outlet to express her pain and run away from the sadness that had enveloped her home, Laurie joined her high school drama club. In an effort to channel her grief, she poured herself into acting in school plays and citywide drama competitions. By her senior year she had won so many awards and drawn so much attention she was approached by several major Hollywood agents. They felt this small dynamo would be perfect for television.

Two months after her graduation, in a situation that read like a script from an old Mickey Rooney movie, she was cast in a starring role in *Name of the Game* TV series. Laurie made her screen debut acting alongside Robert Stack, Julie Harris, and Sal Mineo. A few weeks later a three-page spread in *TV Guide* introduced the teen to the American public. She was an overnight success. Offers poured in, new friends introduced her to a larger role that was intoxicating, and a whirlwind of activity surrounded her every move. The new crowd that was a part of her world urged her to forget about her old-fashioned Christian values. They made fun of prayer and worship. They painted Christians as ignorant, narrow-minded bigots who didn't really understand the world. They laughed at those who attended church or stopped to pray. Over time, Laurie drifted away from her Christian roots. Church attendance became an afterthought, as did reading the Bible. As busy as she was, few could blame her for sleeping in on Sunday mornings.

The next decade was a blur of activity as Laurie leaped from show to show, playing a "wild child" on *Gunsmoke*, working with Rod Serling in *Night Gallery*, appearing with Anthony Quinn in *The Man and the City*, taking on roles in *The Waltons*, *The Incredible Hulk*, and *Testimony of Two Men*, and even costarring with film legend Bette Davis in the acclaimed miniseries *The Dark Secret of Harvest House*. The quality of her performances was such that Tennessee Williams asked Laurie to consider starring in one of his plays. She had become a Hollywood success story, but in the process, she had lost something her father and mother cherished much more than anything else.

"Two years into my career," Laurie recalled, "I remember my father and I having a dreadful argument because I had stopped going to church. He could sense that I was being seduced by the world and my ego was turning me away from my faith."

Joseph had lost one son to a war he had no control over and didn't understand, but he was determined he was not going to lose a second child to a cultural war he did understand. He was going to do everything in his power to make sure God remained first in Laurie's life. When discussions did not work, he and his wife turned to the most important weapon in their arsenal—prayer. They prayed for Laurie on a daily basis. Just as her brother's death drove her to distance herself from God and her family's priorities, it would take meeting and marrying a Christian man, along with another family death, to bring her back home.

Richard was a dynamic singer, a producer, and the head of a record label. He was good-looking, talented, and filled with spirit. That spirit, which Laurie discovered when they began to date, came from his faith. Richard, the first man to fully win the actress's heart, surely had to be an answer to her parents' prayers. When she fell in love with and married Richard, Laurie took a vital step back to her parents' Christian roots. These were to be the happiest days of her life, but it would take a day of great sadness for Laurie to fully understand the incredible power of faith.

"My father had already lost a kidney to cancer," Laurie explained, "but then the cancer came back. This time it was all over his body. When I would visit, as soon as I saw him I would start to cry. All the lost years I kept so much of myself from him, we had had our disagreements, but I never doubted his love and pride in me."

Her father's faith and strength, which he had exhibited in quiet ways throughout Laurie's life, now showed in ways the daughter could not fathom. He was simply not scared of death. As Laurie panicked and sought out miracle cures, reading all she could about cancer, Joseph smiled through the pain and told her how much he appreciated her constant research in looking for the latest treatment to find a cure. But all the study and prayer was for naught. At four one morning, she got a call asking her to come to the hospital to say good-bye.

As she and Richard drove across the city, Laurie was immersed in a cloud of grief. She was hopeless, heartbroken, and confused. She asked God one final time to reach out from heaven and heal her father. God would reach out, but in a much different way than Laurie had anticipated.

"My mother and all of us children were present at his bedside," Laurie explained. "We were all surrounding him, tearfully saying our good-byes. His skin was ashen, his face drawn, and he looked terrible. But at the moment before taking his last breath, his face became so vibrant and filled with such a glow that for a moment I thought he was coming back to us. I will have the look in his eyes imprinted in my memory my entire life. It was absolutely clear to me that he was passing out of this world into a greater life. It is absolutely a certainty to me that the life we live on this earth is not the end."

Laurie had been introduced to faith by her father's and mother's life; she had lost a great deal of her faith when her brother was killed in war, and now she had rediscovered her faith through her father's passing. She sensed God was all around her and that he loved her even when she was living a less-than-perfect life. Yet to fully make the trip back to where her father had prayed she would be, it would take many more years and the influence of another great person of faith.

Being married to a man who produced Christian music, Laurie was often introduced to the latest lyrics of Spirit-filled songwriters. But it was in the works of a long dead writer where Laurie met a kindred soul and found her own gospel voice. That writer was the legendary Fanny Crosby. The positive words found in Crosby's music so deeply touched Laurie that she yearned to know more about the song's composer. She had always been a student, always loved to do research, carefully finding out the background of each of the real-life characters she had played on screen and stage, so plugging into a fact-finding mission was an adventure she relished. Little did she know that reading about Fanny Crosby would be the final catalyst in redirecting her life back to the path her parents had always followed.

Crosby was a legendary hymn composer. In her ninety-five years she wrote thousands of hymns. These songs were so timeless in message that hundreds are still being sung today. Blind since early childhood, Fanny was one of the first with her handicap to overcome the disability and achieve fame. By the time she was forty, Crosby had become an accomplished poet, a best-selling author, an outspoken advocate for the handicapped, a woman who had addressed Congress, and a person who called eight American presidents her friend. Yet none of that could make up for the loss she felt when her own infant child died. In the depths of despair she embraced the faith she had witnessed in her grandmother's life. It was then the door opened for her to give up her secular poetry and write hymns. While she would know great fame for the rest of her life, the fortune she could have claimed she gave away to the poor.

Just as Crosby had strayed from a close walk with God, so had Laurie. Just as the songwriter had found secular acclaim at a young age, so had Laurie. And just as that fame had not brought Fanny great fulfillment, neither had Laurie's time in the spotlight.

"As I studied Fanny's own words," Laurie explained, "I found a road map for my own life. One of the first of her thoughts that hit me was 'Whatever talent one possesses belongs to God—give him the credit.' "

The more Laurie read about Fanny, the more she realized how much the short life of her brother Joey had been spent reaching out to those who had less than he did. She also realized that her mother and father had been that way as well. She began to wonder how many of the kids who had spent so much time at the Pranges' home were now living a solid, faith-based life simply because of the example of love, compassion, outreach, and acceptance they found through Joseph and Evelyn.

Laurie even thought that Fanny had been talking about Evelyn Prange when she wrote that she never judged others but attempted to present to them a better way. Crosby used kind, soft words and gentle prodding rather than harsh judgments to show the lost the way home. It was Crosby's kind, soft words that put Laurie back on track.

For Laurie Prange, the example her father had set and the continuing spiritual influence of her mother prodded her to take a second look at her faith. She began to spend her spare hours developing a project about Fanny Crosby. She wanted to tell the story behind the composer's life, to show that the blind woman's faith went far beyond her music. As Laurie worked, she continued to ask God for guidance. She ultimately found that sometimes you have to get hit in the head to realize that he has been there watching over you all along.

"One night I was unable to sleep and went across to the guest bedroom. As I watched TV I deliberated whether to keep the door open or to close it so as not to awaken my husband sleeping in our room. Though it made no sense, I chose to keep it half open and half closed. Later in the evening I awoke with a start, turned off the TV, got up, and ran smack into the edge of the door."

For Laurie the pain was excruciating, and she was so dizzy she could barely stand. Her husband drove her to the emergency room, where she was surprised to learn she did not have a concussion. What the CT scan revealed was a mass the size of a quarter on her brain. Other tests confirmed that Laurie had a tumor. The tumor would have gone unnoticed for weeks, maybe months, if Laurie had not run into the edge of the door. She felt it was God who had presented that painful lesson as a way of showing how much he loved her and watched over her. Now the question became, was she dying?

"The time between discovery, surgery, and pathology," Laurie explained, "was a window where the realization that I may soon be departing this life was very real. In a sense this tumor, which turned out to be benign, was a gift and put into perspective how precious life is. It helped put into clarity for me what to cut loose out of my life, who to reach out to, and where to put my energies."

The realization of the fragility of life also presented a new reality to Laurie. She understood that being a Christian meant more than just being a good person, praying, and going to church.

"The fact that we are all special and are all of significance and purpose to God means we have a job to do. We were born with a purpose. This life goes so quickly, and each decision we make and each step we take brings us closer to God or takes us farther away from God. Too often in my adult life I had made choices that had put distance between myself and God. Now my prayers are for strength to follow God's will and to make Christ an example in body and spirit each new day."

For Laurie the time to fully embrace the faith of her father and mother had finally arrived. This was her awakening to the fact that the God who had guided her father from life to beyond was ready to take an active part in every moment she lived as well. So on that night, as she bowed her head and repeated what she had so often heard her mother say, "Now I lay me down to sleep," she knew that God had her soul and life in his hands and was not going to drop either of them. All he asked of her was to find a niche and show others her faith through example.

"It took me losing my brother and my father before I truly realized that life is a gift and a privilege. All of us know people whose lives were cut short, and it is for us who remain to do our best to honor this gift of life."

For Laurie this means picking up her brother's work of reaching out to "the least of these," carrying on her father's work of living his faith in word and deed, and becoming a nonjudgmental prayer warrior like her mother—doing things that draw people to her as a woman who has a peace and understanding that they need in their lives as well.

"I struggle with my faith every day. It is not a slam dunk. But the reality that there is a heavenly Father who watches over me *is* a slam dunk! I talk to him every day and ask *him* to take control of my life as I navigate each choice I make. I choose to try to live my life through the eyes of faith rather than through the eyes of cynicism. I have found there is a light in the eyes of those who live with faith, and I want that light."

Though she still acts in television, on film, and in the theater, Laurie Prange's main goal is to bring Fanny Crosby's story to life. She wants the world to get to know the special lady because she feels Crosby's example can lead as many to the Lord as has her music. And in a world where modern men and women are blinded by a myriad of temptations, she feels the blind composer can show them the way to see the true light.

Laurie has seen that light in her mother and in her brother and she even saw it in her father's eyes in the moment he died. With every prayer and every action she knows that her life can be a quiet example to others who are living in the darkness but yearn for that light. She knows, like those who led her to the Lord, that every action is a moment of opportunity. She has become her parents' daughter and is walking in their footsteps as she performs in the spotlight. While critics marveled at her portrayal of Blanche DuBois and of the wild child in an episode of *Gunsmoke*, in truth Laurie Prange's best role began when she found her faith and became God's child.

8

DAISY LOW

Faith Found When All Was Lost

Daisy learned the lesson that God taught Moses: when you allow God to be in charge of your life it's never too late to change the world. While she didn't part any seas, she did provide a road that has positively shaped millions of young women all over the world.

Juliette "Daisy" Gordon Low was forty-one years old and living in London, England, when her world began to crumble. She had been born into wealth in the year prior to the American Civil War, and most of her first four decades of life had been spent on frivolous activities. All that mattered to Daisy, until she discovered her husband's infidelity, were the parties, the summer homes, the shopping trips, and being listed on the social registers of two different countries. As her husband boldly paraded his mistress before her, as loneliness mixed with anger seeped into every corner of her mind, she realized that her own lack of personal substance reflected a life of little accomplishment or value. As she wondered what she had done to earn the pain she was now feeling, she realized all of her good deeds could be listed on a gum wrapper. It was a painful blow. She, a Christian, had never really been a part of God's work. In fact, she had pretty much ignored him.

Daisy was born in Savannah, Georgia, on Halloween Day in 1860. Her grandfather and father had made their fortunes in railroading and banking, and they enjoyed every dollar they made. The Lows lived in a section of the city reserved for the upper class and owned the nicest carriages and the finest horses and wore the best clothes. Even the destruction and havoc wreaked by the Civil War, which had ruined many Southern families, had little effect on the Lows' fortunes.

Daisy spent her grammar school years at home, being doted over by her parents and the family servants. She was sent to a boarding school in Virginia to fully develop the social skills needed by genteel women of the time. From the Virginia Female Institute, she was shipped to Mesdemoiselles Charbonniers, a New York City finishing school. It would be there, mixing with young women from America's most elite families, that Daisy would make the connections needed to become an icon of social sets on both sides of the Atlantic.

Though bright, Daisy never did well in school. She didn't have to. Her personality carried her through even the toughest situations. She was naturally witty, energetic, and confident. Everyone seemed drawn to her. She was also one of the most creative young women in the school. She could come up with an endless list of ideas for parties, socials, and trips. Though she could conceive wonderful projects, she did not have the drive to finish anything she started. She began several efforts in drawing, painting, sculpture, and writing, but very little completed work resulted from these ventures. She simply could not focus on anything but having fun. When she graduated from Mesdemoiselles, she had grown into a very attractive woman, but had little of value, other than her degree, to take home to Savannah.

As was the custom with the city's finest families, Daisy was given a "coming out" party. Her debut was filled with fun, frivolity, and beauty, but the whole extravagant affair was ultimately nothing more than a reflection of the role played by wealthy women in the old South. They were decorations who were never asked to think or work. With people always catering to their needs, most had little connection with the real world. With no job or obligations, Daisy, likes scores of her peers, lived for parties, dances, teas, and church.

Daisy's experience with faith was as shallow. She might participate in a Christmas charity bazaar to raise money for the poor. She could even quote a bit of Scripture when called upon. But living out Christ's directives was an abstract concept she did not understand. In her mind God had chosen for her to be born into wealth, just as he had deemed that others suffer in poverty. She saw little need to reach out to share the blessings she had always known and no reason to mix with those from the middle or lower classes.

Through her social circles, Daisy met William MacKay Low. Low was a handsome man with a European flair to his personality. He knew how to dress, dance, and flirt. He was the heir to a cotton fortune. Though Daisy's parents did not approve of the man, thinking him too wild for their sheltered daughter, the twenty-five-year-old woman adored him. Listening to her heart rather than the counsel of friends and family, Daisy married Low on December 21, 1886. This union of two shallow social butterflies got off on the wrong foot when rice, tossed at the couple as they left the church, became lodged in the bride's ear. The tiny bit of grain would lead to an infection that would cost Daisy a large portion of her hearing. Still, in spite of suffering from partial deafness, the bride could take comfort in being immersed in a life taken from the pages of the romantic novels young women loved. For Daisy there were no limits; whatever she desired she could have.

The Lows split their time between a residence in Savannah's Lafayette Square and an English country estate they named Wellesbourne. On both sides of the Atlantic, Daisy hosted parties where her guests included high-ranking officials from the British and American governments, actors and actresses, writers and artists, industrialists, and even members of the royal family. While her husband gambled, played polo, and joined friends for fox hunts, Daisy shopped at the finest London shops and dined at the world's best restaurants. A regular at Buckingham Palace, the American woman seemed to be at the heart of the British social scene. A party was not an event unless Daisy's name was on the guest list. She was essentially the well-kept wife. She knew it and it was a role she played to the hilt. Besides briefly helping to raise funds for the treatment of wounded men returning from the Spanish-American War, she lived a life that centered completely on herself and her own needs. Ironically, she was so busy with her full social calendar that she never noticed her soul was empty. It was only when she was faced with the fact that her husband had abused her trust that she realized she had no reservoir of faith from which to draw.

Daisy filed for divorce and found herself in a fight for everything she owned. The battle dragged through various English courts for months and might have stayed in litigation for years if William had not suddenly passed away. Free from a man who had wronged her, Daisy then discovered her husband's will left everything they owned to his mistress. In order to hold on to just the property she had brought to the union, Daisy was forced to go back to court. The fight, largely waged in English courtrooms, was a long and trying one for the American woman.

Nearly deaf, childless, alone in a foreign country, and deserted by many of her British friends, the usually outgoing Daisy was all but grounded by depression. As she studied her life and totaled the score, she realized her history had little value. She might have lived among the most famous movers and shakers, but she had done nothing of importance to place herself in that position. She was a hollow forty-five-year-old shell with no skills and no future. Convinced she was too old to find another husband or to have children, she believed she was doomed to live by herself in a world that would be forever shrinking to the point where she would die and no one would even notice. What Daisy did not know was that many of those around her were just as empty and frustrated as she was.

For five years, as she fought to hold on to some of her estate, Daisy searched for ways to spend her days. Just as she had as a child, she would gain a passion for some type of art, dream of becoming the next great master, work at her new craft for a while, then grow bored and give up. When each new fad faded, even she began to realize what everyone else had always known: she was incapable of finishing anything she started.

After five decades, the canvas that represented Daisy's life was still blank. As she studied her past, it seemed to her as if she had never lived a single meaningful moment. Surely God had created her for something, but she wondered if she had simply been too busy partying to notice what that something was. In terms of the way people thought at the time, she was labeled as "over the hill." She was not even on the favored party list anymore. But what about God? Did he still think she might be worth saving? Did he still have a job for her?

Daisy did not have to search her Bible very thoroughly to find that there were many stories of older people who had submitted to God's will and found the time to accomplish great things. Moses was hardly a spring chicken when he was given the task of leading his people. If God could use an old man as a guide, then maybe he could find a place to use an older woman as well.

Until that moment, Daisy Low had always put herself and her wishes first. She had never done anything for others unless she too was going to benefit. She had never even looked for ways to serve. In the Bible she discovered stories of men and women who dropped their old lives to give themselves to new worthy causes. Christ taught that those who really trusted him had to give up all they had to prove it. The great missionary doctor Albert Schweitzer had told an Oxford graduating class, "I don't know what your destinies will be, but I do know that the only ones among you who will truly be happy are those who have sought and found how to serve." For a desperate Daisy, it was time to seek out a place where she could leave a mark on the world.

In 1911, Daisy met Robert Baden-Powell. As the American woman and the English war hero visited, they discovered each had an interest in sculpture. It may have been their mutual love of art that brought them together, but it would be another of Baden-Powell's passions that opened a door of opportunity for Daisy.

Baden-Powell had been the moving force behind the start of the Boy Scouts. Though less than a decade old, thousands of British boys were involved, and the movement had proven to be a great success. The old Army officer saw scouting as a way to not only teach skills needed for surviving and enjoying outdoor life but also as a place where boys from different demographic groups could work and learn together. In the English culture of the period, there were few chances for the different social classes to mingle, so Baden-Powell's vision was seen as a radical new concept. As he had shaped scouting with boys, his sister, Agnes, had begun programs working with British girls. Her Girl Guides, though not as well established as her brother's boys groups, had nevertheless seen solid growth in areas around London.

Daisy's English friends were hardly surprised that she would volunteer to help in the Guides program. The socialite was always eager to begin a new pursuit. Yet her history had shown that after her rapid and enthusiastic start, Daisy always lost interest and gave up her latest venture to try something new. Most of her friends felt this would happen with the Girl Guides. Baden-Powell, a new acquaintance, did not realize the woman he was encouraging to help shape young lives was hardly dependable, so he entrusted her with a chance. That one chance was all she needed.

With her advanced social skills, Daisy had no problem getting to know Agnes and her girls. As a novice at many of the skills being taught by the Girl Guides program, Daisy found she was learning as much as the young people. She loved it. The camping, hiking, and service projects breathed new life into her heart. She was more enthusiastic about the experiences than even the kids were.

After a few months of working with young women in Britain, the American woman grew even more passionate about the potential for the group. She wondered how different her own life would have been if she had been placed in an organization where poor, middle-class, and rich girls had all mingled, working together to learn and perform tasks of service to the community. Sensing it was time to go home and make her mark, a determined and focused Daisy bid ado to Baden-Powell and to England and returned to Savannah.

As soon as she arrived home, Daisy placed a call that would ultimately impact more than 100,000 girls in the next eighteen years. When her cousin picked up the phone, Daisy hollered, "Come right over! I've got something for the girls of Savannah, and all of America, and all the world, and we're going to start it tonight!" Over the next few weeks, all Daisy could talk about was God using her through scouting.

While her friends and family were happy to have Daisy home, most wondered what had happened to her. She was no longer a self-centered social butterfly but instead a woman who expressed a deep faith in God and a desire to use her faith to reach out to young girls in every facet of the community. As she excitedly explained her desire to start a local scout movement, she emphasized how different her life might have been if she had been able to join such an organization. It was this realization that now drove her. She might have wasted a large portion of her life chasing trivial things and not caring about the state of the world, but it was time to make sure a new generation of girls did not toss their lives away.

On March 12, 1912, eighteen girls came together at Daisy's home. The first one to sign up as a Girl Guides member was Daisy's niece Margaret "Daisy Doots" Gordon. While Daisy Doots and most of the other girls had little idea why their mothers had forced them to attend the meeting, the woman in charge would soon make it crystal clear. She told them they were going to create a program based on what she had learned in England. Their group would give girls programs that would help them develop physically, mentally, and spiritually. This would not be a club that embraced only the elite; every girl from every social setting would be welcome. She wanted these first scouts to help her find girls who came from isolated home environments to be a part of this movement. Each new group would get to enjoy camping, recreational activities, cooking, reading, and public service. She finally told the eighteen that what they were starting would in time go to every corner of the globe.

Not fully grasping Daisy's plans for "world conquest," the girls were nevertheless almost as excited as their leader. Their joy was in knowing they would get to go camping. Activities like that had generally been reserved for boys. They also felt it was going to be fun to be a part of something imported from England. None of them envisioned that they would be the foundation of an organization that would someday claim millions of members worldwide.

Daisy Low's vision of exposing girls to a wide variety of activities and service opportunities was more important to her than any of her friends could imagine. This was not just something she was using to fill her time; she saw scouting as having more potential for good than any other youth organization. She saw scouting as a way to show young people not just the wonder of God in nature but the joy of doing charity work in their own communities. Although she had no plans to make her scouts a licensed Christian group, she was going to make sure that God was at the heart of each element of the work. Therefore, in subtle ways, the Christian character and spirit of service she had lacked for more than five decades would become part of each scout's essence and fiber. With that in their hearts, they would make their world a better place than the one in which she had grown up.

For the first time in her life, Daisy's interest for a project did not diminish with time. As she taught the initial scout groups in her hometown, she laid plans to take the movement to the whole country. As she pondered the best ways to accomplish this goal, she began to see God's hand on what she had considered her wasted years. While active in the social set, hosting dinners and attending lavish parties, Daisy had met some of the wealthiest and most powerful people in America and England. Her personality and wit had charmed them. These people genuinely liked Daisy. Thanks to her years mingling with the world's most famous people at mindless social events, she now had the contacts for financial support and press coverage.

With her original Savannah group, now called Girl Scouts, actively involved in camping, sports, and civic projects, and with a number of new chapters being started in and around the city of her birth, Daisy made an East Coast tour to explain her vision to her influential friends. She even wrangled a visit to Congress and the White House. She designed uniforms, outlined a list of accomplishments to earn higher rankings and honors, and composed a manual to be used by each girl in every troop. Near the beginning of her first scouting book she wrote these words, "We, the members of Girl Scouts of the United States of America, united by a belief in God ... believe that the motivating force in Girl Scouting is a spiritual one." Thanks to her relentless promotion and newborn faith, within a year of founding her initial troop, thousands of girls in the United States were being led by hundreds of volunteers.

Over the next eight years Daisy continued to travel to every corner of the nation, pumping up the importance of expanding the work. Yet she did more than just talk about the movement she began; she remained an active, hands-on leader. She continued to go on hikes, boat excursions, camping trips, and cookouts. She performed community service projects with her troops. She even studied and took the tests to earn various merit awards. She was not just a leader, she was a true Girl Scout.

As she continued to spread the word, churches were among her greatest allies. Congregations recognized that scouting gave the churches a way to touch segments of their communities they had often been unable to reach. Inviting girls from the community into the houses of worship for scout meetings also reinforced something Daisy believed was an essential part of her vision: scouting was God's work. In fact, scouting was what he brought to her when she felt she was too late to make a positive impact.

Viewing scouting as her calling, Daisy wanted to expand her group to reach the very "least of these" in every corner of the world. Scouting, she preached, will show people how much they have in common and how much they can accomplish by working together. She felt the movement would help eradicate prejudice and anger while creating a new generation of socially conscious and disciplined female leaders.

In 1923, the tireless Daisy realized she was a step slower than she had been just a year before. For the first time she was having a problem keeping up with her girls. At first she blamed it on age, but pain drove her to visit a doctor. An examination revealed she had cancer. There was nothing medicine of the time could do for her. Not wanting to burden anyone with her own problems, she kept the diagnosis a secret and maintained her demanding workload. She vowed to push scouting until she could walk and talk no more.

For the next three years she traveled worldwide, speaking to groups, raising money, leading troops on campouts and hikes, and constantly explaining to those around her how lucky she was that God had given her this wonderful calling. She did not stop her efforts until January 1, 1927. A few days later Daisy received a telegram from the national officers of the organization she had founded. "You are not only the first Girl Scout, you are the best Girl Scout of them all." On January 17, holding the telegram in her hand, she died.

Daisy Low's funeral was held at Savannah's Christ Church. She was buried in a scouting uniform. As her body left the church, hundreds of the city's Girl Scouts, dressed in their uniforms, lined the steps, standing silently to honor the woman who had given them a chance to learn, grow, and experience the joys of God's world. Around the country, more than 100,000 other Scouts stopped to honor her as well.

Almost a century after Daisy held her first meeting in Savannah, more than four million girls are involved in Girl Scouts. One of the most recent troops was formed in the middle of Africa's worst slum. These girls from Kibera, Kenya, who have lived in squalor and filth, are now being elevated by scouting and will soon learn the story of Daisy Low. They will be taught how this woman looked to God for a second chance to use her talents, and how he gave her a vision that led to millions of women making an impact all over the globe. Daisy Low's story proves that it is never too late to change, and that no one with faith is too old to lead that change.

9

DR. ANNE BROOKS

Faith Heals

Told that a crippling disease had effectively ended any chance she had to go into the world and actively serve God, Anne had to fight not only her illness but a world of doubts before she could bring the healing touch of faith to a forgotten and hopeless people. Few women have done as much with so little.

When you begin to write about a person having inspiration, hope, faith, and compassion, where do you begin? When you point to a person living out Matthew 25:35–40, how do you trace the roots of that pattern of service? Why can one person endure pain, suffering, and anguish and turn them into a life of dynamic and positive outreach?

Dr. Anne Brooks went to the Mississippi Delta knowing she would never make any money. She knew from the start that only a few patients would be able to pay her anything at all. She realized that she would live the rest of her life as a poor country doctor. But Dr. Brooks also felt the Delta was where God wanted her, and she eagerly gave herself to the very least of these who live in America. Her unusual path to her humble clinic began when, as a child, she observed another woman stooping to perform a task many would have considered beneath them.

"I'll be right back," eleven-year-old Anne Brooks shouted to her playmates at the Florida convent school. "I'm going upstairs."

Climbing the steps of the dormitory, Kitty, as Anne was known to her friends and teachers, rounded the corner and stopped in her tracks. Through the bathroom door, she spied a nun on her knees scrubbing one of the toilets. Shocked, Kitty ran through the door and grabbed the woman's arm.

"Get up!" she cried. "This work is not for you. This is dirty work."

Wiping her hands, Sister Henri Ferdinand stood and took the dismayed, blonde-haired girl in her arms. After holding her for a few moments, the kindly nun said, "Kitty, there is no dirty work when you work for God. The Lord told us that 'if you have done it to the least of these, you have done it to me.' We take care of you because he wants us to. This work is part of taking care of you. What I do, I do for you and for him."

Kitty couldn't believe what she had heard. As a self-centered only child, she had never even considered doing things for other people. Staring into the nun's chocolate-brown eyes, the girl, for the first time in years, felt loved and wanted. In that moment she experienced her first inkling of what agape love really was.

This revelation of what it meant to give yourself to following Christ took place more than five decades ago. At that moment America was still savoring the victory in World War II. It was that war that had separated Kathryn "Kitty" Brooks and her mother from her father, a navy officer. During that four-year conflict, perhaps as a result of loneliness, Kitty's mother became an alcoholic. Soon after the war ended, so did her parents' marriage. When the decree was signed, Kitty was taken from her mother's home in Washington, D.C., to be near her father's naval base in Florida.

Because he could not take care of her while serving, Kitty's father placed her in a Catholic boarding school. Knowing nothing about the Catholic faith, the girl obviously felt isolated and unhappy in the dorm she shared with twenty-nine other displaced girls. Most of her roommates felt as she did: unwanted and unloved. For most of what seemed like endless days, Kitty was adrift. Life held little meaning. But on that afternoon in the dormitory bathroom, lightning struck. She suddenly had a role model, a hero, someone who accepted and loved her without any restrictions, boundaries, or borders. For the first time, Kitty realized she belonged to a family and she sensed it was the family of God.

At that moment, as if she had been given a message from heaven, Kitty began to dream about being a nun and being wrapped in his arms just as she was wrapped in the arms of her teacher.

At age thirteen, Kitty Brooks converted to the Roman Catholic faith. Following graduation from high school, she trained to become a nun. She hoped to fulfill a life of service working with people. She worked toward that with every facet of her being. She prayed daily to be completely used by God as his servant. Her teachers marveled at her energy and enthusiasm. They all predicted great things for the very bright teen. Then tragedy hit with such force that it seemingly ended her dreams and put her life on hold. When she was eighteen, Sister Anne Eucharista, as she was now called, was forced into a wheelchair by rheumatoid arthritis.

Like the first blast of winter, the disease came out of nowhere. There didn't seem to be any indications that the incredibly healthy and active young nun was anything but the picture of health. With both parents dead and no family of her own to turn to for help, she seemed destined to waste away behind the walls of a home for retired nuns, her dreams of service dashed by a vicious disease that easily claimed her vitality.

After examining Anne, each in a long line of doctors shook their heads in agreement. Her situation was hopeless. They could offer no solutions, no exercises, and no means for her to escape either her wheelchair or the pain that gripped her like a vise. Given no hope of ever getting better, she finally accepted her illness, but that did not mean she was going to sit around and do nothing. She convinced her supervisors she could still work and talked her way into a position teaching fifth grade students at the Academy of the Holy Names in Tampa, Florida. For several years things went well. Then, in 1960, Anne's illness decided to squeeze her even harder. One day as she picked up a piece of chalk, pain raged through her body and she was unable to lift her arm to write on the chalkboard. Reluctantly, the principal considered moving her to bookkeeping and records. Essentially the young woman was being retired, put out to pasture like a farm animal that no longer has much value. Frustration set in and was soon followed by depression. Anne had become a nun to make a difference in people's lives, and now, relegated to sit in a lonely room studying files, she was no longer directly touching lives. Though she was young in years, her body was aging at a rate she couldn't begin to comprehend.

In the face of ever-worsening pain, Anne would not give up. Even when her superiors urged her to give up her work, she pushed to do more. Feeling more and more trapped by her disease and the way it limited her world, she jumped beyond her limited role at her school and volunteered to work twice a week at a free health clinic. The job was limited to after-school hours, but to the nun who so wanted to serve others, it was like a breath of fresh air. Just touching the hands of poor people, who had no money and little hope, drew Anne closer to her Lord. If all she could do was pray with them or make them feel as if someone cared, it allowed her to feel as though she was doing a small part to live out Jesus' command to reach out to the "least of these."

One evening, looking out over a waiting room filled with scores of almost lifeless faces, Anne studied those waiting for a bit of release from the pain of a desperate life. There were frail old people, drug addicts, and tiny babies held by homeless mothers. She understood them. They had no money, no other recourse for medical care. She knew that many of them at one time had been employed and had done well. But for whatever reason—loss of a job, death of a spouse, an addiction to drugs—they were now on the bottom looking up. They seemed to have no hope. She could see in their eyes that many had given up. They no longer had dreams. They just lived out daily nightmares.

Realizing these people blamed God for what was happening in their lives, Sister Anne decided there had to be a way for her to visibly show them the love God had for them. Maybe, she decided, if they understood it wasn't God's fault their lives had gone sour, they would turn to God again. But how, she wondered, could a nun in a wheelchair perform this kind of miracle? What kind of example could she pull from her own life that would give these people hope and restore their faith? Anne prayed daily for answers, but it took two years of patient waiting to understand that God was listening to her pleas.

In 1972, the founder of the Clearwater Free Clinic, Dr. John Upledger, a specialist in osteopathic medicine, looked at Sister Anne and said, "You know, you don't have to be in such pain. You can get better."

Stunned, Anne turned her head and whispered, "What?" If someone other than the kind doctor had spoken the words, she would have dismissed it as a cruel joke. But Dr. Upledger's tone indicated he was serious. If that was the case, then why had she been told there was no effective treatment for rheumatoid arthritis? How could this doctor believe differently?

Upledger, a tall, heavyset figure with gray hair, intense blue eyes, and an expressive face, sensed Anne's confusion. Smiling, he asked the nun a question that revolved around her own faith and perception of the Lord. "You don't think that the God you serve so willingly wants you in pain, do you?"

This question had never come up. She had accepted her pain as a cross she must bear. It was a part of her life. She had grown to believe it might even be a test. She had never considered getting over it or even fighting through it.

After considering the man's question, in a resolute tone she demanded an answer. "How can I get better?"

"For starters," the doctor explained, "you have to believe that God *can* make you pain-free. Do you believe he can?"

Anne considered the question for only a second. If God could part the Red Sea, if he could create the world, if he could heal the blind man and raise the dead, then he obviously could erase the pain from her life.

"Yes," Anne replied, "he can."

"Then he will," Dr. Upledger pledged. "Then he will."

After again smiling at his volunteer, Dr. Upledger said, "Ninety percent of getting better is believing that it is possible. First, we've got to look at what is causing you stress, what eating habits you have that need improvement, and what's not right with your bones and muscles. Then, with God's help, we can make you pain-free."

With Dr. Upledger guiding the way, the sister realized her frustration at being unable to provide the clinic's patients with sufficient help had been bothering her and causing her even more stress than she felt just being locked away from people doing books. In fact, she was frustrated with almost every area of her life. She was stressed because she felt she was not doing enough to fulfill her vows to serve. She realized that she was bringing most of the stress into her life. Anne began to use quiet times for prayer and meditation. Following her doctor's orders, she used those moments to turn over to God the pain she felt for others. She devoted more time to her earthly temple and got into the habit of eating balanced, low-fat meals at regular intervals.

Day by day, with help from osteopathic manipulation of the joints and muscles, plus acupuncture treatments and exercise, she became more and more mobile. The wheelchair that had confined her off and on for more than a decade was pushed into a corner. Free and happy, feelings of bitterness behind her, Sister Anne became the clinic's most vital healing instrument, dashing around at light speed, a smile lighting her path. Just like her teacher who had scrubbed toilets, the nun relished the chance to fall to her knees and clean up places where people had vomited on the floor or to carry lice-infected children in her arms. She was sure she had found her calling and that the rest of her life would see her in such service. Little did she know this was just the first step of a journey that would have been impossible to imagine.

In 1975, Dr. Upledger left Florida to teach at Michigan State University's College of Osteopathic Medicine. Soon after he settled in, Sister Anne visited him for a checkup. When he met her at the airport, Dr. Upledger said, "Anne, you've got to become a doctor."

"John, you're nuts," the nun replied, laughing.

"No, I'm not. Imagine, Dr. Sister. Imagine what you could do. Imagine what your life could mean to so many."

"You're still crazy," Sister Anne shot back. "I could never be a doctor. I don't have any science background or, more importantly, any money. Don't forget, I took a vow of poverty."

"You're not going to let a little thing like that stop you, are you?" the doctor fired back. "After all, it wasn't long ago that people told you that you'd spend the rest of your life in a wheelchair. Look at you now. Listen, Anne, you have what it takes to become a doctor. If you believe that as strongly as I do, we can find the money to get you through school."

Over her time in East Lansing, Anne considered her physician's words. The more she turned them over in her head, the less they sounded like a joke. Maybe, she thought, even with the odds against her, she might just be able to make it through the school. When she left the campus to attend a retreat in New York, she promised Dr. Upledger she would pray about his challenge. At the retreat, a deeply thoughtful and somewhat confused Anne asked the director how to know if God wanted her to become a doctor.

His simplistic response almost stunned her. "It's easy to know what you should do," he assured her. "If you are on the right path, the doors will open."

Back in Florida, Sister Anne learned about the National Public Health Corps. Under that program, the federal government would pay the full cost of medical school for any student who promised to serve in a depressed area after graduation. Anne applied and, to her delight, was accepted. Not only had God answered her prayer for funds but he also assured her he had a special need for a middle-aged doctor sister.

Medical school was fraught with pressure. For a woman who had not been in school in years and whose health was frail at best, it was a monumental challenge. It took almost as much prayer as it did studying to get through each semester. Yet class by class, challenge by challenge, the nun moved forward. In a very real sense, she became an inspiration to her younger classmates as well as a spiritual mentor to all around her. Her success, she explained, was due in part to her efforts to look at her problems from God's perspective. That helped her appreciate how really small they were. Even more valuable, she explained, was her belief that she was doing what God wanted her to do. With her positive attitude, the reams of information she was required to learn seemed to flow more easily into her head. Still, when she passed her boards and earned her license, it seemed as if the Red Sea again had parted. In Anne's mind it was that kind of miracle, and it served as proof that with God's help and a little faith, anything is possible. In June 1982, Sister Anne received the diploma that signified her new status as a doctor of osteopathy. She thus became Dr. Sister Anne Brooks.

Now that the question of if she could become a doctor had been answered, she wondered where God would lead her to use her new skills. The answer to that question was already in her head; she just had to tap into the memories of a trip she had taken the year before.

In 1981, Anne had driven her old Plymouth throughout the South. The trip had been made to look for a town that might accept a nun who hung out a medical shingle. She avoided the tourist spots along interstates, choosing instead to travel winding two-lane, black-topped ribbons of asphalt connecting towns filled with empty store buildings and people with few options for upward mobility. In the Mississippi Delta, she took a map and a medical directory and marked all towns with hospitals and doctors. She noticed that one, Tutwiler, had neither. Prayer presented her with a call, so she wrote a letter to the town council. When the mayor read her letter, in which she stated she wanted to move there voluntarily, he thought it was a joke. The last doctor had fled that tired town and its 1,200 poor, mostly African-American residents thirteen years before. He had gotten tired of not getting paid and living an existence that offered him no chance at ever living any of his own dreams. After barely scraping by for several years, he just up and left.

When Anne arrived in town to meet the locals, a council member warned her, "We don't have a golf course and no place for a doctor's sailboat. Nobody has any money. All we have to offer is a lot of people who need health care."

What Anne thought was the answer to her prayer was a dying town in the heart of Tallahatchie County, fifth poorest county in the nation. Money was so tight that officials had turned off the town's lone stoplight because they couldn't afford the electricity to run it. As Anne walked down the lonely streets, she was greeted by the faces of skinny children with empty eyes, old people consumed by the effects of malnutrition, and former cotton pickers whose bent backs were frozen with osteoarthritis. Even before the mayor showed her the spacious clinic building that had been empty since the mid-1960s, Sister Anne knew she had found the place she would practice. To her, it was as if the Lord was saying, "Anne, here's your clinic. I was just saving it for you." When town officials offered to lease the building for one dollar a year, Sister Anne promised she'd be back as soon as she completed her internship.

When she returned, Sister Anne discovered that she constituted the entire Catholic population of Baptist Tutwiler. Some townspeople were concerned that she might try to start a Catholic church. Sister Anne immediately put their fears to rest. "I'm a healer, not a preacher or a missionary," she assured them. In a few weeks they would find that, like God, Anne saw all of these people as his children and therefore her brothers and sisters. Rounding up three other nuns to help her, she rented a house and begged and borrowed medical equipment. Finally, on August 15, 1983, the doors of Tutwiler Clinic opened.

Since day one, the clinic has had no budget. It just runs, mostly on reimbursements from Medicare and Medicaid and whatever fees patients can afford. Sister Anne quickly discovered that, while most of Tutwiler's citizens are desperately poor, they are proud people who want to pay their own way. If they can't do it with money, they bring in catfish or garden greens or offer to sew or to wash pill bottles. Whatever payment was offered, she gladly accepted the gift as if it were pure gold.

One day the doctor received a note from a pregnant teenager whose life she had saved. As she read the unpolished correspondence, Anne felt like the richest physician in the world: "Doctor Ann—I am gonna to pay. I just an't had no money but I a show gonna pay your because if it was not for your I would be dead today."

A few weeks later, an elderly woman with Elephant Man's Disease limped through the clinic's door. All Sister Anne could do was to give the woman, whose name was Mary Sue, some free medication to relieve the pain. To pay for the medicine and services, Mary Sue made a quilt for Sister Anne. The gift warmed not only Sister Anne's bed but her heart as well. And it gave her an idea. With encouragement from the sisters, Mary Sue and others began a quilting circle. The women began selling their carefully sewn, colorful quilts to pay not just for health care but for other badly needed items. Their growing independence did wonders for their self-esteem.

The more patients they treated, the more the sisters realized that the people's needs were not just health related. Many couldn't read and few had a high school diploma. They were not equipped to compete in a modern world. Drawing upon their educational background, the sisters set up classes after clinic hours to teach basic skills.

As donations began coming in from concerned people around the country, Sister Anne and her staff, which now numbered almost twenty, were able to open a clothing exchange that also handled emergency food requests, to launch a program to prevent teenage pregnancy, and to begin a play program for two- to four-year-olds with mandatory parenting classes. In addition, the sisters stimulated the formation of the Tutwiler Improvement Association, which has sponsored town cleanups and Christmas parades and is changing attitudes so that townspeople now work together on various civic projects.

One evening, when she returned to the clinic to teach a class studying for the state General Educational Development (GED) exam, Sister Anne looked in on an exercise class. There, in the middle of the huffing and puffing, she saw God. These overweight women were sharing in a dream—self-improvement—and now it was becoming the dream of everyone in the community. They had a need, and they had asked her to fill it. It dawned on Sister Anne that the need she had felt as a child—that hollow pain of not being wanted or needed—was long gone. In the middle of the nation's poorest people, she had gained a wealth that money can't buy.

In the evenings, Anne often listened to classical music. One night as she was praying, she remembered a sister who had considered Sister Anne to be wonderful because she was a missionary in Mississippi. She had smiled at the compliment and asked the nun, "Just what is a missionary?"

"Someone who brings God to the people," was the quick reply.

Sister Anne didn't agree. "The Lord lives in my patients here, just as he lives in everyone everywhere. If I help people to recognize their own dignity, then I increase their ability to see the workings of the Lord in their own lives. They grow closer to him, even as I do by coming in contact with them. So you see, I'm not in Mississippi to bring God, I'm here to find him."

The once-crippled nun first understood love and service when she observed a teacher on her hands and knees scrubbing commodes. The lesson she learned that day was that no work is beneath God's people. He challenges all Christians to stoop and reach out to the least of these. Little did she know at that moment that she would become one of the sick, the poor, and the helpless before she would find her prayers answered and could fulfill Matthew 25 in ways she never could have dreamed possible. All it took was realizing the God who parted the Red Sea still works miracles today.

10

HELEN CORNELIUS

Faith to See beyond the Pain

When she was spinning country music hits in the 1970s and 1980s, Helen's voice was regarded as the sweetest in Nashville. Yet this woman's most lasting impact would not be a No. 1 record, but rather a rocky journey that began with grief and ended with understanding.

In 1985, forty-year-old Helen Cornelius, one of country music's brightest stars, was enjoying a rare day off. She was sitting on the couch in the living room of her home at the foot of Rattlesnake Mountain, twelve miles south of Nashville, Tennessee. The summer sun shone through a large picture window, the rays highlighting her blonde hair and making her green eyes sparkle. This rare solitude brought a peace that she had rarely experienced. She was relishing the moment when one of her sons entered the room.

"Come here, Mom," nineteen-year-old Joey pleaded. "Come over to the piano and sing 'The Rose' for me. Of all the songs you sing, you know it's my favorite."

Flattered that her teenage son wanted to hear his mother sing, Helen smiled and immediately jumped up from the couch. She hurried across the room to the gleaming black grand piano and sat on the bench next to Joey. Placing the tips of her fingers on the ivory keys, she played the opening notes of "The Rose," a song made popular by Bette Midler in the 1979 movie by the same title. Then in a soprano voice accented with a soft southern drawl, Helen began to sing: "Some say love, it is a river that drowns the tender reed."

As his mother sang that bright afternoon, Joey's face lit up. Seeing him happy caused Helen's heart to surge and her mind to wander.

"Where have the years gone?" she asked herself. In her mind, Joey was still a blond-haired boy running across pastures, not this young man who was trying to earn a living by riding bulls in the rodeo.

Joey, the eldest of her three children, had just started school when Helen's songwriting first wowed Nashville in the early 1970s. It didn't take long for Music City to discover her vocal talents. In 1976, she and Jim Ed Brown had become the most successful duo in the country music industry. Most thought their reign of hits would last for decades. Yet after four strong years that featured sold-out crowds and gold records, Helen made what many thought was a career-killing move: she opted to star in a touring road show of a Broadway musical. It was a huge leap of faith, jumping into a genre that had nothing to do with country music. Most predicted certain failure. Shocking all but her closest friends, Helen won rave reviews touring the nation in *Annie Get Your Gun*.

When the tour ended, the woman who had been pigeonholed as a duet partner, but not a solo act, put together her own band and started performing more than two hundred concerts a year. The product of Hannibal, Missouri, was far more successful than she had ever dreamed, yet just when it seemed her career was about to really soar, she cut back. Always one to pray, she felt God was asking her to spend more time with her children. On this day, singing to an audience of one, a son who obviously was proud of his mother's talent, she knew she had made the right decision. This one moment with Joey was worth more than the applause of five thousand.

At a time when most children pushed their mother away, Joey tried to make spare moments for Helen. He wanted her to know how much he loved her and appreciated her support. For him it seemed especially important to have her realize he was determined to be the best at what he was doing. And, knowing what was most important to her, he was going to work as hard as she did to become the best Christian he could be. He had no idea how much his faith lifted her spirits.

But she was a mother and she wanted to push him in directions she felt were best for his life. Helen hated the fact that Joey put his body at risk in a rodeo arena. With every ounce of her being she wanted to hog-tie him and keep him home. Yet she could no more do that to him than her own mother could have kept her from moving to Nashville to fight the uphill battle in the music business. So instead of begging him to give up something he loved, she simply told him again and again, "Joey, I love you. Please don't ever get hurt."

"I love you too, Mom," Joey replied. "Please quit worrying. I'm not going to get hurt. I will always come back home to hear you sing."

A few days later, on July 10, 1982, Helen was sitting on the back porch with her fifteen-year-old daughter, Christie. They quietly talked as they watched the sunset when a guest shouted, "Helen, Denny's on the phone! He sounds upset!"

Rushing into the house, Helen wondered what her younger son wanted. Then she remembered he had gone to the rodeo to watch his older brother ride bulls.

"Denny, what's wrong?"

"Mom, I'm at the hospital in Lawrenceburg. Joey's been hurt. You better get here fast!"

The trip to the hospital took two hours. Denny met them in the lobby. Helen grabbed her thirteen-year-old son, looked into his eyes, and asked, "Is your brother all right?"

Trying hard to be brave, the boy shook his head.

"Is he in surgery?"

Again her son shook his head.

"Well, I want to see him." Running to a nearby doctor, she demanded, "I want to see Joey! I'm his mother!"

Leading her into a large room, bathed in harsh overhead light, the doctor gently pointed to a sheet-covered body lying on a hospital gurney. Helen stared for several moments, tears welling up in her eyes. She could not fathom nor believe what she saw. Finally, without moving, she broke the awkward silence by whispering, "Is he dead?"

The doctor nodded.

"He can't be!" Helen cried. "He just can't be!"

Helen collapsed in the arms of the closest person and screamed, "This can't be true!"

After she regained a bit of her composure, the doctor said, "I'm sorry. He was too banged up for us to do anything. He had extensive internal damage. When a boy gets thrown from a bull and then ..." The doctor's explanation drifted off. She didn't want to know the details; all she wanted to do was turn back the clock. As the physician continued to speak, the shock set in and Helen's mind went blank.

During the week of Joey's funeral, Helen lived in a fog. Not once did she acknowledge to anyone the pain she felt over the loss of her son. Most of those around her thought she was so strong. They whispered to each other how Helen's faith never wavered. They marveled at how Helen could find something good in every bad thing that happened.

Internally Helen mirrored the feelings of others. She felt that her well of faith would pull her through. Yet as the days slowly moved forward, she learned the death of a loved one, particularly the accidental death of a child, can try the faith of even the strongest Christian. Instead of expressing her grief and turning to family and friends for comfort, Helen felt it was her responsibility to demonstrate strength and to comfort them. In an effort to lift her family's spirits and take their minds off Joey's death, Helen decided, one week after his death, to go back on the road. She was scheduled to perform at the Wheeling Jamboree.

She seemed a tower of strength when she set out for West Virginia. Yet as she got closer to the venue, she suddenly felt weak and alone. She also began to blame herself for Joey's death. "If I hadn't become a country singer, Joey would have never fallen in love with the rodeo. He'd be alive!" As guilt came crashing down, she surrendered under its weight. She now believed her choice to be an entertainer had directly led to her son's death.

Helen made it to the performance, but she was not in good physical or mental shape when she arrived. For a week she had faked strength, but that night it was obvious to friends that her state of mind was as fragile as glass. Even though the promoter told her to take the night off, she refused to listen. "You're on," someone shouted. Helen took a deep breath, crossed the stage, and waved to the enthusiastic crowd. As the cheers subsided, she sat down at the piano. She had never felt so alone. Where was God? Where was her faith? Why was she here? What can I do? Then, not understanding why, she began to play "The Rose."

As she pushed the piano keys, a strange hush fell over the huge throng that had gathered that night. And when Helen's voice quietly and soulfully embraced the song's opening passage, every eye focused on the tiny woman in the middle of the huge stage. As she embraced each word, squeezing the emotion out of the lyrics and mixing it with the pain in her heart, the audience hung on her every word. Afraid to make eye contact because she feared she would break down, Helen stared blankly into the sky. For those in the audience who had recently experienced their own grief, and especially for the many fans who knew of Helen's loss, the words of the chorus took on a profound new meaning. It was as if Joey's adventuresome spirit had somehow come alive. The line "And the soul, afraid of dyin', that never learns to live" told the story the audience needed to hear, but it left the singer awash in grief.

Helen, now overcome with emotion, struggled bravely through the second verse of the chorus. When she reached the end of the song, with its powerful message of hope, the crowd remained strangely silent. A few seconds later, when the spell was finally broken, fifty thousand spectators erupted into a standing ovation. Many could not hold back the tears. Acknowledging the adulation by rising and giving a slight wave, Helen rushed from the stage, tears streaming down her face. She returned home immediately, unaware of the tremendous healing impact she had had on many in the audience.

Despite the outpouring of love from her family, friends, and fans, Helen couldn't shake her grief. During the weeks that followed, she withdrew from everyone, even her children. When the tears didn't work, she turned back to an old habit: prayer. In her prayers, Helen begged God to give her understanding as she pleaded again and again, "I've been a good Christian, Lord. Why did you take my Joey away?"

When she didn't receive an answer, Helen went back on the road, trying to work herself into forgetting, or at least masking, the pain. Like so many facing the loss of a loved one, burying herself in her craft became her way of escaping.

To keep Joey alive, Helen began to talk about him on stage at her concerts. Speaking from her heart, she explained the light that her son had brought into the world. She spoke of his faith, his goodness, and what he meant to her. Then, after explaining how much he had loved "The Rose," she would sing his favorite song.

After her concerts, Helen was shocked when her fans lined up to tell her what her Christian witness and love for her child had meant to them. It seemed that Helen's belief that Joey was with God had strengthened their faith. Dozens of men and women told her that, because of her message, they had turned their lives over to the Lord. Ironically, instead of consoling or uplifting her, these testimonies actually pushed Helen further from reality. As more and more people told her what an incredible woman of faith she was, the more she resented the role. Yet she felt she had no choice but to "fake" her way through it.

For several months, whenever anyone asked her how she felt, she smiled and answered, "I feel wonderful and life is just great." In truth, she was falling apart. Even as she said all the right things on stage each night, deep inside she questioned why, if those around her thought she was so strong and had all the answers, was she still experiencing so much pain? Though not seen in public, the anger building up inside Helen began to be exhibited in outbursts directed at her family and her band.

One day, almost two years after Joey's death, an elderly woman asked Helen for her autograph. As Helen signed the photo, the woman told her, "Your strength has meant so much to me. I find it easier to deal with my own heartaches because of how you have dealt with yours. You are a godsend, a real angel."

Smiling, Helen handed the woman the autograph, but the woman's words left Helen so cold she vowed this would be the last time she would ever live this lie of faith. Her son was dead; he was not coming back. And the pain was so bad it made her want to never be close to another person. With that attitude she marched back to her tour bus to have it out with God.

At the end of her rope, Helen glanced over at the mirror. Staring back at her was a worn-out imitation of strength, an angry shell. She knew the charade was over. Sobbing, she whispered, "Yes, Lord, I believe in you, and I know that Joey is with you. So if I understand and accept all of this, if I read my Bible and pray all the time, why can't I feel good? Why can't I release all my grief and guilt?"

For two years she had tried to find the answers all by herself. None of the pat formulas she had used as a child had worked. She had said the right things and imitated the right people, but she was still angry. And then there was the big joke of everyone thinking she had all the answers when she didn't have a clue. She wanted to give up. She even tried that for a few days, but it wasn't in her nature. So like any lost person should, she finally stopped and asked for directions.

Sitting in her pastor's office, Helen revealed the big lie she was living. The man listened to her story and then gave her this advice: "Helen, you seem to think that by denying your grief you demonstrate that you are a good, accepting Christian. Even the one Man who lived a perfect life felt pain. Until you begin to deal with Joey's death, your hurting will not end."

Helen began reading her Bible even more intently. This time she was not just rushing over the words; she was looking for meaning. One day she stopped at Philippians 4:13: "I can do all this through him who gives me strength."

"That's it," she thought. "I may not understand everything, but I can do something. As a Christian, I have a power within me that not only sets me free but also helps me. I've been ignoring it, trying to depend on my own understanding and strength. It isn't Helen who makes me strong, it is the Lord."

At that moment, the bubble that had been insulating Helen from reality began to crack. She began to feel both the pain of loss as well as the joy of renewed life.

She knew that her not wanting God to have Joey or her failure to understand why he was taken from her didn't make her a sinful person. Finally, she understood that it's okay not to understand, and that failure to understand didn't make one a failure.

"God has given me the ground and the seed," she explained. "It is up to me to plant it, till and water it, and keep it growing until he decides it is time for the harvest. The soil in my heart is rich, and God's promise of support is strong."

Sensing that allowed Helen to finally acknowledge that she had done what God had wanted her to do with Joey. Her son was not only everything she wanted him to be but everything God wanted him to be too.

It has been two decades since Joey died. Helen is still touring as a country singer and inspiring others with this message: "I would have given anything to have saved Joey's life, but I now realize there was nothing I could have done. I still miss him, but when I struggled through the period of trying to show the world and God that I am a worthy Christian, and that I understood why my son had to die, I began to realize that I'd never fully understand. What I have come to understand is just how much love the Lord has for each of us.

"I thought I had loved my children more than any parent in the world. I wanted to protect them from every heartache and every one of life's traumas. I never wanted them to feel pain or doubt or to have to struggle with questions. I expected a lot from them, and they couldn't always live up to my standards. Yet, even when I was disappointed, they knew I still loved them. As they grew older and began to make their own decisions, it was time for me to back off and love them differently. I realize now how painful that can be.

"God too is a parent. He loves me even more than I loved Joey. God asks me to try to follow him and trust him. I try, but I have fallen short of his expectations countless times. Yet, he continues to reach out and assure me that he loves me. I had been so intent on trying to earn God's love that I failed to realize his love is as free as the love I had given my own children. God only wants me to do my best.

"I don't have all the answers. But I now know that not having them is okay. I feel God's power every minute of every day. This doesn't mean that life is always easy. It just means that I have a parent—the Lord—who is beside me, helping me through the tough times.

"I still feel the pain, but I no longer hide it in my heart. Now, when people I know suffer a loss, I assure them it is all right to hurt, to question, to grieve. Then I share with them God's promise of tomorrow.

"I have found that losing someone we love is sometimes a way for us to realize the real miracle that is life and the real power that is love. Joey's life gave me so much, but his death gave me something also. I have a much greater understanding of the depth of God's love.

"I now share every part of my life, both the good and the bad, with God. I treat him the same way I want my children to treat me. I can't be perfect, and I can't control the heartache of life. But the power to survive, and then to grow and love again, is within me. As long as I remember this, I can balance the pain with love and joy, and I will never again isolate myself from God."

In each of her performances, Helen still pauses to sit at the piano and sing Joey's favorite song. When she reaches the line about "under the bitter snow," she understands the beauty of the rose is just a prayer away. Thanks to her loss and her struggles in working through it, as well as the faith that bloomed from the pain, thousands of others have come to know the soaring truth she found when she hit rock bottom. She has fully learned the meaning of the last line of Joey's song, the meaning that eluded her for the two years she suffered through anger and doubt: "And the soul afraid of dyin' that never learns to live." Helen Cornelius is relishing each moment of life again.

11

MOTHER TERESA

Faith Filled with Compassion

The path of life was rocky for this humble nun. For so much of her life, no one predicted great things for this woman, yet the fact that she lived most of her life as an overlooked outsider in a strange land forged the monumental faith that would inspire the world.

We have all known people who seem bent on living impossible goals. Many of these idealistic dreamers embrace causes that leave them forever swimming upstream. They ignore the pleas of friends and family to take the practical route and to stay on the proven road. Nothing can discourage them even though it seems obvious they are bound for ridicule and failure. It spite of the odds, there is something in them that pushes them onward. Eventually, most give up, defeated, discouraged, and disheartened. Only a very few hold on to their dream and keep pushing forward. They are the ones who know that even though it may appear they are struggling alone, God is always with them.

A tiny woman, born into a cultural mixing bowl in Yugoslavia, would certainly fit into the parameters of those defined as impossible dreamers. Yet what separated this woman from millions of others who embraced goals that seemed unreachable was that she knew why she was doing it; she understood from where her call came, and she made the impossible in her life possible. Ultimately, millions were dramatically changed by her fortitude, conviction, and faith.

Gonxha Bojaxhiu was born in Skopje, Yugoslavia, on August 27, 1910. From her first breath, she was considered a minority. Her roots labeled her an Albanian, her family raised her as a Catholic. She was one of the few of her kind living among the Slavs, Muslims, and Orthodox Christians who populated the region.

Gonxha, or Agnes as she was called by most of her friends, was the youngest of three children of Nikola and Dronda Bojaxhiu. Her father owned a construction company and the family was prosperous enough that they had not one, but two homes. They essentially lacked for nothing. They had clothing, food, and funds for entertainment and education. They were well-read, engaged in the local community, and respected in their church. In a world filled with abject poverty and social unrest, this family was middle-class and stable. Yet if there was a sticking point in their lives, it centered on Nikola's fascination with politics. He loved to debate issues and often took positions that placed him at odds with those in power. His courageous and unbending stands on local social issues probably were his undoing. In 1917, after meeting with men who opposed his views, he grew suddenly ill and died. The Bojaxhiu family was sure he had been poisoned, but local officials failed to take action. Still, even without their breadwinner, the family, led by their mother, continued to live at a level few in Skopje could manage.

Agnes was a small, shy girl who nevertheless had a deep curiosity about everything around her. She loved to study history and was especially fascinated with the stories of men and women involved in the early missionary movement of the Catholic church in Europe. Agnes also delighted in visiting with her Catholic teachers about the current efforts of evangelism. A student of the Bible, she recognized how the past and present work of missionary outreach related directly to the teachings of Christ. Again and again she pointed out how these heroic men and women were living out what Jesus told his disciples. Even though she lionized those who spread the gospel, at no time during her formative years did she show any bent to pursue a life in Christian service. Like most teen girls of the period, she was much more focused on dreams of courtship, weddings, marriage, and children. Yet as she finished her high school studies and looked into the future, she made what many at the time thought was an impulsive decision. She decided to travel to Ireland to study education at a school for novice nuns. Few in her community could begin to fathom this sudden change in course, much less how the frail girl would ever stand up to the rigors of international travel. They figured she would be coming home within weeks of her departure. Most would never see the girl again.

Just as most had predicted, Agnes was completely unprepared for life at the Loreto Sisters of Dublin. The convent school, founded in the seventeenth century to educate young girls, was a completely foreign world for the tiny girl. She spoke little English, knew nothing about the local culture, and did not have a full grasp of the expectations of her teachers. But Agnes, more than any other student at the school, felt as if she had been called to be a minority in a strange world, so she rallied on. Being the only one of her kind at Loreto Sisters no doubt helped to prepare her for the country and work where she would make her mark.

For one year, Agnes was basically alone. She struggled with her English, was constantly homesick for family and friends, and fought to develop a taste for Irish customs and food. Her teachers found her ordinary and predicted little would come from this student, while her fellow students thought her strange and far too serious. However, in the face of this adversity, the calling Agnes had felt when leaving her home grew stronger. Her commitment and self-discipline grew more resolute, as did her belief she was to spend her life in Christian service as a missionary.

In 1929, the novice nun was sent to Darjeeling, India, to teach at a school that was supported by the Sisters of Loreto. Two years later, after finishing her studies and choosing her new name, Sister Teresa was sent to St. Mary's, a high school for girls in Calcutta.

In a very real sense, for the next seventeen years nothing set the nun apart from her peers. She was just another nun who taught the daughters of local wealthy families behind the protective walls of St. Mary's. During this period she advanced from classroom instruction in history and geography to being named the school's principal. But there was nothing in her actions that forecast any greatness. While she noted the poverty and despair outside the St. Mary's campus, she did not actively respond to it. As the years went by, as she began to grasp the great division between those she taught and the children who begged in the streets, she committed more time to prayer, seeking to rationalize this divide. Over time, the fact she was not being an instrument to "the least of these" began to eat at her soul.

On September 10, 1946, Teresa was riding on a train. As is still the case on Indian trains, her car was crowded, uncomfortable, and noisy, making her situation feel claustrophobic. All around her were poor, needy people. Many were from the lowest level of the caste system and were considered untouchables by the children at her school. Outside her window, as her train stopped at stations, she could not help but witness lepers begging on the platforms. Their condition created such great ridicule that most Indians cursed them at every opportunity. As her journey continued, it seemed like every poor person in the nation was looking into the nun's face and asking for help. The experience would be unsettling for even the most hardened soul; for the caring nun it was a noisy ride through hell itself. In the midst of the numbing, chaotic distractions, Teresa heard a voice speaking to her. Because no one else was hearing this voice, she was sure it belonged to God and he was speaking directly to her.

Teresa would later explain that the voice told her to quit her life as a Catholic school principal for the Sisters of Loreto in order to live and work with the poor in Calcutta. Though some of her fellow sisters doubted that Teresa had really heard God's voice, the tiny nun simply could not ignore what she was sure she had heard. She resolutely explained to the doubters, "It was an order. To fail it would have been to break the faith." Yet for a while, because she had to follow church directives, she could not march out the gates of St. Mary's and follow her Savior's demands.

In the weeks that followed, she heard his voice dozens of times. On each occasion she was given the same vision of reaching the poor in Calcutta. These commands were the strongest during times of worship and prayer. Over the next few months, the words heard only in her heart provided her with a blueprint of a great ministry in the city's slums. The scope of this mission would dwarf anything being attempted by any organization at that time, yet the only person who seemed called to create and maintain it was Teresa. None of her fellow nuns was interested in going beyond St. Mary's gates.

The nun wrote to Calcutta's Archbishop Ferdinand Périer. She informed the church leader that Jesus wanted the "Sisters of Charity to be my fire of love amongst the very poor, the sick, the dying, the little street children." And who were the Sisters of Charity? For the moment, they numbered only one. Not committing to this vision, Périer told Teresa to continue her duties as the school's administrator while he and others studied her proposal.

For twenty-four months the tiny nun waited, growing more and more frustrated with her inability to respond to God's call. During this period it became more difficult for Teresa to focus on her duties at school. She continued to write letters outlining her vision, and she heard God's voice repeatedly urging her on. Finally, on August 17, 1948, after her proposal had been caught in the church bureaucracy for two years, the thirty-eight-year-old nun finally received the archbishop's blessing. Within minutes of being authorized to start her own mission work, the nun left the security and safety of the school's grounds to first take a course in nursing and then to hit the unruly and dangerous streets of Calcutta. With no money and armed only with her faith, the woman was once again alone in a foreign world. As she told those concerned with her safety, "If we have our Lord in the midst of us, I fear nothing. He will look after us. But without him I cannot be—I am helpless." As she would soon prove, she may have been underfunded and undermanned, but she was anything but helpless.

India was a nation long subject to colonial rule. Therefore a majority of the nation's people had little trust in foreigners. As the country was less than 1 percent Christian, missionaries were often greeted with disdain and even violence. The streets of Calcutta were hardly a safe place for an armed British soldier, much less a diminutive Catholic nun. If Teresa felt fear, she didn't show it. She marched confidently into her world of calling without even looking over her shoulder. She knew scores were staring at her with hate written on their faces, but she was sure that when they saw the love of Christ in her heart, she would win them over.

God had told Teresa in her vision that she needed to start her work by reaching out to the children of the slums. Though she had no building, she began a school in an alley. Gathering street children, she taught basic skills by writing with a stick in the dirt. It was her chalkboard. Though she was actually smaller than many of the abandoned children who made up her school's student body, she appeared larger than life to her waifs. No one had ever shown them anything but contempt. They had grown up digging through trash for food. They had no clothes but what they wore. Until she started her street school, they also had no hope for an education. The tiny nun was therefore a friend, a mother, and a beacon of hope.

Those in the surrounding community viewed the woman's work with the children with great suspicion. Many felt she was trying to overthrow the nation's time-honored caste system. Others thought she was going to somehow abuse the children she was helping. Politicians even questioned if she was trying to start a revolution. In a sense she was, but like Christ, the definition of her new "kingdom" was initially misunderstood. She was not involved in overthrowing a government; she was, in reaching out to the world's "least of these," showing the love and the message of Christ. That is what she tried to tell all who questioned her mission.

As Mother Teresa explained it: "Christ wants to give us the chance to put our love for him in living action. He makes himself the hungry one, not only for bread but for love. He makes himself the naked one, not only for a piece of cloth but for that understanding love, that dignity, human dignity. He makes himself the homeless one, not only for the peace of a small room but for that deep sincere love for the other. This is Jesus, the Living Bread that he has come to break with you and me."

In trying to live Matthew 25:35–40, she used her street school as a base to reach the adult community. Slowly she made her way to the homes of poor families living in squalid shacks. They expected her to try to convert them to her faith. While this was her ultimate goal, she first inquired about their needs. When she heard their requests, the nun sought help in filling those needs.

Within months of leaving St. Mary's, Sister Teresa was helping hundreds through modest programs committed to educating children as well as feeding and clothing the poor of all ages. Yet even though she was saving scores of lives, making a dent in the massive poverty and need in Calcutta was literally impossible. There were too many starving and naked children, too many lepers, too many elderly, and too many mothers who had nothing. The nun found herself swimming upstream, battling just to keep her head above the water. It was an exhausted Teresa who each night literally collapsed into the small bed in her tiny slum apartment. Gaining little help from Christian groups while facing continuing hostility from the established Hindu society, a lesser individual would have given up. After all, anyone could see this was an impossible mission. Teresa's faith never wavered. She had always been an outsider, a minority, a person different than all those around her. God had prepared her well for being by herself doing his work in Calcutta. If she had to go it alone, she would.

As the nun continued to struggle to establish her work, she spent more and more time alone on the streets working with the city's poorest people. On one of her treks she spotted a sick woman sitting in the dirt, her body covered with open wounds that had become infested by parasites. The small nun helped the woman to her feet and gently cleaned and dressed the oozing wounds, the elderly woman fighting her every move. Despite being cursed and pushed away, Teresa continued her work until every sore had been cleansed.

When the nun got up to leave, the ungrateful woman yelled at her, "Why are you doing this? Who taught you?"

Teresa smiled and explained, "My God taught me."

"Who is this God?" the sick woman demanded.

The nun smiled, leaned over, and kissed the woman on the forehead. "You know my God. My God is called love."

Even the Christians who witnessed these compassionate acts could not fathom why the nun would continue this exercise in futility. It was obvious that few she touched actually appreciated her efforts. So, they asked, why didn't she just go back to the safety and security of St. Mary's?

"When Jesus came into the world," she explained, "he loved it so much that he gave his life for it. He wanted to satisfy our hunger for God. And what did he do? He made himself the Bread of Life. He became small, frail, and defenseless for us. Bits of bread can be so small that even a baby can chew it, even a dying person can eat it. Just as Jesus allowed himself to be broken, to be given to us as food, we too must break, we must share with each other.

"The shut-in, the unwanted, the unloved, the alcoholics, the dying destitutes, the abandoned and the lonely, the outcasts and untouchables, the leprosy sufferers—all those who are a burden to human society, who have lost all hope and faith in life, who have forgotten how to smile, who have lost the sensibility of the warm hand touch of love and friendship—they look to us for comfort. If we turn our back on them, we turn it on Christ, and at the hour of our death we shall be judged on whether we have recognized Christ in them and on what we have done for and to them."

In reaching out to the poor, not only was Teresa following a calling, she was following the Bible. She was doing unto the poor as if they were Jesus himself. As a formerly suspicious Hindu student explained it, "Sister Teresa took Jesus' words on faith—that he would remain with us truly until the end of time, that he would come to us in the bread and wine we offer on the altar, and that when we look into the eyes of the hungry, the homeless, and the unwanted, we'll find his eyes looking back."

During the first two years on Calcutta streets, as she fought to establish her own mission, Teresa struggled financially and suffered hostility from even those she was trying to help, but she never thought of giving up. Though her work remained small, reaching only a few people, her faith was making an impact. One by one, local individuals came forward to see if they could help her. Young women were the first to volunteer, and though few were Christians when they came to offer aid, these women would become the first nuns who made up the Sisters of Charity. Soon men and women from wealthier areas offered food, clothing, the use of buildings, medical supplies, and money. As her mission grew beyond even her vision, she told those who marveled with her, "I am God's pencil with which he writes what he likes." In her case God was writing a masterpiece of love and compassion.

The rest of the work of the woman who would come to be known as Mother Teresa is well documented. Her ministry touched millions and her energy and drive to reach the poor were never diminished. She became an Indian in the way she dressed and thought. The country that was once suspicious of her grew to claim her as one of their most revered citizens. For fifty years she gave every moment of her life as a response to the call she had heard on a train traveling across India.

On September 5, 1997, Mother Teresa, a woman who had started life in obscurity in a tiny village in eastern Europe and lived to grace the cover of *Time* magazine, finally ended her work for God on earth. Even in death she placed the importance of the Lord above everything else. Those who wrote her obituary quickly discovered that the task had been made much harder because of certain actions the nun had taken in living out Matthew 25:35–40. To make sure God's work was not lost in her own celebrity, she had long before destroyed her notes and had requested that her friends and colleagues dispose of letters she had sent to them. "I want the work to remain only his," she told them. Nevertheless, a few of those letters remain, and some reveal a very human woman who remained devoted to God's work even during times when she experienced great personal doubts. This surviving correspondence will no doubt bring great assurance to many who suffer through similar dark days as well as provide inspiration for scores to continue their work during these bleak times.

The woman who became a legend as Mother Teresa began her great work as someone who believed that with God's help the impossible could become a reality. Because this woman was unafraid to swim upstream, to challenge conventional thinking, and to go beyond the walls of security, tens of thousands were saved and millions of lives were changed. She saw God in everyone she met, and they saw him in her.

"The poor are the hope of mankind," she explained, "for in them we see the hungry Christ looking up at us. Will we refuse him?"

Teresa once toiled alone. Now there are thousands following in her footsteps.

12

SARAH CLARKE

Faith Taken to the Faithless

Sarah found her calling not through her husband's wealth, but through service to men and women who joyfully and enthusiastically wallowed in depravity. Little did she know that her mission would provide the light, hope, and faith to save a vile sinner who would become one of the greatest evangelists of her time.

The smell of stale beer, sweaty men, and dirty horses filled the air on that hot summer afternoon in Chicago in 1877. Big men with huge appetites were wandering from establishment to establishment, determined to spend their day in lusty pursuits that would make even a hardened sailor blush. The saloons, gambling halls, voodoo parlors, and brothels lining the stretch of shoddy streets from Van Buren to Twenty-third were a bustle of sinful exploits that broke almost every commandment faster than one could count from one to ten. In this horrid and unholy place, a section of the Windy City even policemen avoided, one small woman slowly and deliberately made her way up the dusty streets. This solitary figure, pushed forward by immense courage and protected by only her faith, looked past the scores of sins that were being committed all around her. Her mission was not to spotlight or judge the multitude of wrongs she witnessed, but rather to open darkened hearts to the light offered through Christian faith.

On this day, Sarah Dunn Clarke was forty-two years old, stood less than five feet tall, and weighed only ninety pounds, but by any measure she was a giant of faith. Though her husband was a real estate magnate with property holdings all over the United States, and even though Sarah was considered an important member of Chicago society, at this point in her life she had little interest in wealth or status.

In fact, she spent more time at a small Christian mission feeding the poor than she did enjoying her grand home in Morgan Park. With a diligence and determination unmatched by even the city's most recognized pastors, the diminutive Clarke sought out "the least of these" wherever she went. Her message was simple, "God loves you and so do I. Leave your old life behind and follow the Lord."

Because she worked on the "wrong" side of the tracks and sought no publicity, most of Chicago's "proper" and well-to-do Christians knew nothing of Sarah's work. The few who did occasionally accompany her to the facility for poor children and women at the corner of South State Street and Twenty-third Street or watched as she walked down the sordid skid row streets were awed by her need to put her faith into action. Even when the poor overflowed her mission, Sarah seemed to believe there was more she had been called to do. To find that calling she visited with men whose lusty natures and disregard for common decency struck fear into the hearts of even the city's biggest cops. Few, other than this little woman, believed even one of these slimy reprobates would ever climb out of the gutter long enough to take a bath, much less let Christ clean their soul. Sarah unswervingly believed that some of these foul-mouthed, drunken scoundrels had the potential to become a mighty chorus for God, and that someday their combined voices would transform Chicago's skid row into a lighthouse for the world.

The playground of sin she roamed in 1877 was a long way, both physically and spiritually, from Sarah's birthplace in Cayuga County, New York. Protected and pampered, Sarah grew up in a Christian family that taught complete abstinence from the lures of alcohol, gambling, and tobacco. The Dunn family did not allow cards or liquor in their home and did not associate with anyone who did. As she had never seen much of the world, Sarah's beliefs were at best abstract. She had no knowledge of the sinful and lusty nature of unsaved people, and she had no understanding of the power of either sin or faith. In a very real sense, she was vain, self-centered, and focused only upon joys and fulfillment to be found in her own life. Anything beyond her small world was not a concern. In this sheltered and tightly controlled environment, Sarah grew up with a basic knowledge of God, but no real direction for her faith.

In the days just before the Civil War, Sarah was a young schoolteacher. When her parents moved west to Waterloo, Iowa, in 1861, the unmarried woman eagerly quit her job and joined them. Because of her family's position and money, Sarah quickly found herself deeply involved in Waterloo's society functions, attending and helping to host many teas, club meetings, and parties. She sought out the finest clothing and found ways to be seen with Waterloo's most refined people in an effort to be viewed as being at the top of the city's social ladder. Sarah soon became a star in the city's proper social circles and reveled in that status.

Besides keeping an eye on the latest Paris fashion trends, Sarah constantly searched for ways to bring the finest in furnishings and decorations to the Dunn home. It was vitally important to the woman that visitors perceive every room in her house as reflecting the upper-class status she sought to project each moment of every day. In fact, Sarah had such a knack for decorating, she was often called upon to help others get their homes ready for parties. Her creative juices flowed during these experiences, and she always found just the right look for each occasion.

So it seemed strange that on a quiet spring afternoon Sarah was having difficulty completing work on an elaborate table centerpiece in her family's parlor. She had spent a great deal of money on the display, and, even with a fine array of items gleaned from the city's nicest shops, she was still unable to design anything that created a sense of awe and wonder. No matter what she added or how she turned it, the display didn't work. As she studied her handicraft for the hundredth time, she thought, "This is not going to impress anyone." As impressions were so important to her life, Sarah was deeply frustrated.

The next few minutes were spent in silence as Sarah tried to tap into her full range of creativity. Unable to come up with any new ideas, she suddenly found her mind adrift, thinking about everything from the previous night's supper to upcoming events at church. A clock's chiming awoke her to the reality of the moment as well as to the still unfinished centerpiece. "I need more time," she whispered to herself as she listened to the clock tick.

"Time for what?" came a reply.

Glancing around the room, Sarah searched for the source of the voice. No one was in the room. She was still alone. "Indeed," she said, "time for what?"

As she considered the hours she had wasted on the centerpiece, she began to contemplate what she had accomplished in her more than three decades of living. She could quote some passages from famous books, recite a bit of poetry, and recognize the latest in fashion and decorating trends, but that was about all there was to her life. Ultimately, when her mental accounting had been completed, when she had totaled all her accomplishments, Sarah realized her world was filled with little more than social functions and church, and she received little substance or value from either. "Is this all there is to life?" she wondered.

As she turned and studied the various items she had so carefully placed in her family's home, her mind took her back to a drunk she had once seen struggling to walk down the road. He had been lost, but she hadn't stopped to help him find his way. Then there was the man who had lost everything he owned through gambling; she hadn't cared about him at all. And there were *those women* whose occupation was something of which no proper lady spoke. Sarah had proudly avoided sharing the gospel message with them. In fact, each chance she had been given to help the world's most needy, she had run the other way. She had hidden from every opportunity God had given her.

"Time." Sarah Dunn whispered the word again. "It is God's most precious gift and I will squander it no more." Leaving her centerpiece as it was, Sara decided to waste no more of her precious time on frivolity, but to instead focus on sharing God's love with people other Christians avoided. She was no longer going to live in a dirt-free world. She was going to find her way to the filthy places where sin thrived. Those invited to her future parties would never appear on any social register.

Within two years of that moment in the family parlor, Sarah moved to Chicago. Banding together with several other Christian women, she formed a Sunday school on the edge of the toughest section of the Windy City. Most of the funding for this mission came from the women's own bank accounts. Reaching out to abused wives and abandoned children, Sarah distributed food and concern while also sharing the gospel story. As the small ministry grew, Sarah began to go to the business community seeking additional funding. It was on one of these visits she met a forty-three-year-old real estate tycoon. She not only received a nice donation but a new last name. In 1873, George Clarke married Sarah Dunn and they moved into one of the nicest homes in the city. Yet even after their union, Sarah left that huge house each day and traveled back to her mission to share her newfound wealth with those she called "the least of these."

George quickly discovered he could not keep his wife from her calling. That Sarah felt a need to reach those who were avoided was one of the things that had initially drawn him to her. Yet he couldn't help but worry about his tiny bride as she traveled down Chicago's most treacherous streets. He grew so concerned for her well-being that whenever possible he made those treks with her, carefully observing as she pointed out the men and women who so needed God's grace. To George these people seemed barely human. Initially he felt little pity for any of them. Yet as he watched his wife pray for hours, as he saw her try to share the gospel with these desperate souls, he began to get caught up in her mission. Soon he was not only donating more of his hard-earned money to Sarah's cause, but more of his time too.

What Sarah most wanted was a place in the middle of skid row that could be hers. She wanted to bring God to this mission. She wanted this mission to be located where brothels, saloons, and gambling halls thrived. Amazingly, her dream went beyond sinners finding grace; she actually believed that within the walls of the mission at least one sordid soul would be transformed into a Christian worker who would dramatically change the world for Christ. For weeks she prayed for God to give her such a place. Time dragged by and no address was revealed to her. Undaunted, she continued to pray in her home in Morgan Park, on the train that took her to skid row, and even as she walked through the sordid streets of the city's Levee District.

One of the most notorious venues in the Windy City was called Hinky Dink's (no connection to the famed restaurant of today). It was an unsavory place that appealed to the very worst of Chicago's outcasts. In the late summer of 1877, Sarah's prayers for a mission were answered when she and her husband were notified a small store just a couple doors down from Hinky Dink's had closed. This was right where she wanted to be, in the middle of the Windy City's most sin-filled streets.

On September 15, the Clarkes opened what became known as "Colonel Clarke's Mission" at 386 South Clark Street. This rescue mission featured a pump organ that barely worked, a few benches, and just enough space for forty people. Sarah carefully arranged the sparse furnishings and painted verses of Scripture on the building's walls. George realized he could no longer allow his diminutive wife to shoulder the vast burden of this work. It was simply too dangerous. So he retired from his real estate and investment business to join Sarah in full-time Christian service. Together they walked the streets, convincing a few drunks and gamblers to join them at the mission, and then they preached the gospel. With saloons on every side, it was often hard for the Clarkes' message to be heard over the riotous banjos and pianos, but they did not give up.

With George no longer working, the husband-and-wife team was forced to sell many of their belongings to finance their work. For Sarah, giving up all she had for God meant nothing. For her husband, who had labored so hard building up his wealth, letting it go was harder. But as he observed his wife pray, as he watched the joy she received each day ministering to the world's greatest sinners, as he became immersed in her mission to go into places even the policemen avoided, he too caught her gospel fever. Even if it meant selling the mushrooms out of their yard, which they often did, George willingly became an eager partner in Sarah's life calling.

Over time their diligence and work paid off as more and more men staggered through the door to hear what was going on at "Clarke's" place. A few drunken visitors sobered up and gave their hearts to the Lord. Three years after opening on South Clark Street, the Clarke mission moved to a larger facility at 100 East Van Buren. Even before the couple threw open its doors, famed evangelist Dwight L. Moody came to see the Clarkes and their new building. As he studied the old "Pacific Beer Garden" sign that still sat atop the structure, he laughed. He is said to have told those around him, "Only the Clarkes would have the kind of vision to turn a saloon into a house of worship." After Sarah took Moody on a tour of what was to become the new mission, the world-famous preacher suggested the couple keep the old sign, mark out the "Beer," and put the word "Mission" in huge block letters. The new gospel outreach center would open a few days later as the "Pacific Garden Mission."

For the next six years the Clarkes welcomed all types of sinners into their garden of worship. Hundreds came forward during that time, many not just professing their faith but also dedicating their lives to Christian service. Former crooks and gamblers went back into the levees and witnessed to their friends. Some even left Chicago and took their testimonies across the country. Less than a decade after Sarah's first mission opened, this oasis in the middle of the saloons was making an impact beyond skid row.

As most men worked six days a week, it was Sunday that offered many their only chance to fuel their darkest passions. On what was supposed to be God's day, the skid row streets were filled with some of the roughest characters in the Midwest. One Sunday afternoon, as he had on many other occasions, the shortstop for the Chicago White Stockings professional baseball team joined his teammates for a round of merriment. This time the players happened to stroll past the Pacific Garden Mission as a service was being conducted. Pausing for a moment, the young shortstop listened to a song his mother had once sung. Waving good-bye to his friends, but assuring them he would catch up with them later, the man wandered into the mission so he could hear the rest of the old hymn. After the song ended, the guest took a seat in the back of the chapel and listened to an ex-gambler and counterfeiter named Harry Monroe give his testimony. As he sat in the back, he noted a tiny woman who was not just praying with these coarse, ill-kempt men but was also frequently stepping between them to stop fights. He could not believe her courage, nor could he fully comprehend why she would place herself in harm's way just to share the gospel with people who might well have been too drunk to understand her words. She looked so out of place that he never expected to see her again. Yet when he came back on Monday, Sarah Clarke was there to greet him and to pray for him.

Over the next few days he learned from mission regulars that this tiny woman spent a good portion of each day not only maintaining order at the mission but visiting barrooms and prisons. She even had the courage to take fifths of whiskey away from drunken longshoremen on the Lake Michigan docks. Mission regulars told the shortstop that Sarah would go into hell and face Satan himself just for a chance to save one poor soul from eternal damnation. Though he still didn't understand why she did what she did, the ballplayer did respect Sarah's courage and determination.

A few nights later the ballplayer came back again. As he listened to the message and sang the songs, he suddenly understood the driving force behind Sarah's life of service. The power of God filled his soul and he felt the Lord's hand on his heart. He stood up and walked up the aisle of the Pacific Garden Mission. Not only did the shortstop accept Christ as his savior that night but he also decided to follow Sarah Clarke's example and share that message with others. The baseball player would give up the game he loved and soon be recognized as the greatest evangelist of his time. Thanks to a stop at the skid row mission Sarah Clarke founded, Billy Sunday discovered his calling and dramatically changed the world.

Sunday was just one of several great Christian leaders who found the Lord in the mission built by Sarah's faith. All of these men entered Sarah's house as sinners but departed as sober men of God. Clarke's legacy began with Billy Sunday and the other men who left the levee to take Christ to the world. Today, almost 150 years after she gave up designing a centerpiece in her family home, Sarah's Pacific Garden Mission is reaching hundreds of thousands each year with medical care, food, clothing, housing, and counseling. A mission radio program beams around the globe, and after-school programs reach kids who otherwise might join gangs. The once-tiny mission, opened to reach out to the Windy City's most vile citizens, is now known around the world as a beacon for Christian outreach and compassion.

Sarah Dunn Clarke spent almost half of her life dwelling on enjoying the finer things while climbing society's ladder. Then, with a single tick of a clock, she realized the value of time. After this defining moment, the rest of her life was spent bringing compassion and hope to the hopeless while praying her work would make an impact beyond the skid row environment she had chosen as her mission field. Such was the power of her faith. Sarah Clarke prayed prayers so powerful that they are still being heard and answered today.

13

REBA SMITH

Faith in a Still, Soft Voice

Reba was a simple woman who seemingly had little but faith. Yet it was this grandmother's life lessons that would help begin a church building movement in the twenty-first century. While trying to reach her granddaughter, this woman set in motion a song of faith that is still touching millions long after her death.

As a rule great women of faith don't try to call attention to themselves. They usually just attempt to reach out and quietly touch one life at a time. They try to share their faith in such a way as to save a soul. Yet it is their vision — that perspective that allows them to see the potential in those around them — that has started movements that lead to thousands or even millions being touched in incredible ways.

Reba's story is really the story of thousands of grandmothers who took the time to share their faith through life lessons. These nameless, faceless, and usually overlooked servants of God probably have done more to fulfill the Great Commission than all the preachers in the history of the planet. They have been the backbone of faith, the consistent thread of compassion, and the link between vastly different generations. And just because they are unknown does not make them any less important than those now heralded in books on faith.

"Hurry," Clark McEntire urged his four children. "The bus will be here any minute." The rodeo roper and full-time rancher had inherited the job of breakfast chef when "Jac," his wife, took a job as secretary to the superintendent for the Kiowa School District. Clark was a great cook, but his sleepy-eyed children rarely noticed. They were too busy trying to wake up.

Quickly finishing the last bites of their breakfast, the three older McEntire kids scurried around the kitchen gathering up their books and jackets. Grabbing lunch boxes and homework papers, the trio raced against the clock to get out the door. Meanwhile, little Susie impatiently watched the action while warming herself by the fire. The blue-eyed brunette was not old enough to go to school, but in a way, she was just as much a part of this frantic scene as her brother and sisters. Every day she got up at the crack of dawn to eat breakfast, then scurried to get dressed as quickly as she could. She too waited for the big yellow school bus and rode with the other children over the dusty back roads of Oklahoma. Unlike her siblings, her destination wasn't a school building filled with teachers and books and lessons. In her mind she was on her way to a more exciting place, the modest home of her grandparents.

Little Susie McEntire would stand beside the mailbox with her brother and sisters and wait for Gene Wilson to pull up in his old yellow bus. She would peer into the morning haze and listen for the familiar sounds of the well-worn muffler and sniff the air for the first smell of exhaust smoke on the cool morning breeze. When she spotted the big yellow beast lumbering up the dusty road, her heart would leap with joy. She couldn't wait for it to arrive at their little rural home.

Susie would lean toward the road as the bus drew closer, squinting her eyes to see how many kids had already gotten on board. She would stand on her tiptoes, poised to run as it pulled up to the McEntire mailbox. Then, after the brakes had ceased their groans of protest and the noisy door had grudgingly opened, her older sister Reba would help her climb the four steps to the aisle.

"How are you doing this morning?" Gene Wilson would inquire as his youngest passenger made her way past his seat.

"Fine," Susie always said with a smile.

"Are you ready to go?" he sometimes asked as he closed the door.

Susie would nod her head, indicating what her sparkling eyes already showed. She would plop down in the nearest empty seat and look excitedly out a window. Then the cheerful driver, his sharp eyes once again glued to the road, would slowly ease out on the clutch and direct the vehicle back onto the rural route. For Susie, a great journey had begun. All around her, sleepy eyes, large yawns, and bored looks defined both the early hour and the lack of excitement that most of the children felt. To most of the riders, the school bus was only a method used by the state to ensure that all of Oklahoma's children were tortured, twisted, and molded into something foreign and strange called "students."

But the littlest McEntire saw the bus as a means of taking her to the most wonderful place she had ever known. She could hardly wait to reach her destination. To Susie the bus driver was not some hired villain—he was a knight in shining armor, a hero who was delivering her to the most magical place in the world, her grandmother's house. Unlike the others, she never prayed for snow to block the roads, nor did she look forward with great anticipation to the holidays when school was closed and the buses didn't run.

Forty years later, looking back and remembering those early years, Susie said, "I was four years old and I hadn't started to school yet. But almost every morning I would ride the school bus from our house to my grandmother's. It must have been about ten miles."

For a small child, a ten-mile trip must have seemed like a very long journey. With all the stops the bus made, it sometimes took almost half an hour. Many four-year-olds would have been terrified. But this was a ride that Susie loved, time she treasured because of the rewards that came at the end.

"I'd get on the bus in the morning and ride to Grandma's house. The bus would stop to pick up my aunt, my mother's younger sister, who wasn't much older than us. She would get on the bus as I got off. She was going to school, but I was going to Grandma's. As soon as I got off, I'd run up the lane, go inside my grandma's house, and stay with her all day."

Reba Estelle Smith didn't live in a fancy home and she didn't have money to buy her little granddaughter the latest dolls or toys. What she had was grown in her garden, raised on the small family farm, or made with her own hands. The fact that her grandmother was poor and owned very little didn't bother Susie. In fact, she didn't even notice.

What did matter was that Grandma Reba possessed a heart larger than a Rockefeller's bank account. In that huge heart she had saved a vast amount of love that could be freely drawn upon by her grandchildren's requests. When it came to attention and affection, hugs and kisses, time and love, little Susie McEntire had access to an unlimited credit line and special one-on-one service. One quick look at this formula and any of today's best child psychologists would tell you that Reba Smith understood just what every child needs and wants. What would have surprised many of these experts was that she knew this several generations before it was ever written down in books.

"Every morning when I would get to her house," Susie recalled, "Grandma would have hot cocoa made for me. It wasn't some prepackaged powder you'd mix in a cup of hot water. It was the real thing—I mean with the sugar and the cocoa and all that kind of stuff—the kind that always had a film on the top. It was a lot of trouble, but she always did it for me.

"When I got off the bus, I'd come into the kitchen and find my cocoa. I could hear her down at the barn gathering the eggs. Sometimes she'd sneeze when she got a whiff of hay or something, and I could hear her all the way up at the house. She had so many things to do, but she'd always make that cup of hot cocoa for me before she'd go down there. So I always felt that I was much more important than her work."

When she spent her days at Grandma Smith's, Susie never lacked for things to do. There were chores as well as songs and stories. She got to iron handkerchiefs and wash dishes in a pan of hot, soapy water while standing on a flour can. Susie never could understand why her grandmother always washed them again. Even with all this work, there was still plenty of time for sitting on the porch and discussing the fabric of rural life. Grandma never tired of answering Susie's endless queries, the same ones that had plagued curious little girls for generations. Reba treated this bright, energetic child's questions as if they were the most important ones ever asked. Patiently, with the utmost care and tenderness, the tall gray-haired veteran of sixty years of life would share with her granddaughter her wisdom as well as the time-honored traditions of farm life.

"Looking back on it now," Susie recalled, "I saw the love of Jesus through her in the kinds of things she took the time to do with me and for me. When it got too hot to sit in the house, I can remember sitting on the porch. They didn't have any air-conditioning, so we'd sit out in the swing. During this time she would take the cream that she'd gotten from the cow, and after she'd strained the milk to get it, we'd sit out on the porch with a gallon jug and I'd help her churn it. It was the same rhythm as when you'd rock a baby. We would just rock back and forth with a gallon jug of milk in our laps. Then we'd take it into the house, skim the butter off the top, and put it in a bowl. On other days, when the season was right, we'd get a pear off the pear tree. She'd cut it a piece at a time. The first one would be for me, and then the next for her, and so on.

"There were times when it seemed that she'd work all day down in the garden. She had a huge garden, and in the afternoon we'd hoe. Then, after we had worked a while, we'd go out and we'd draw water from the well in a bucket. It'd just be so cool. They had their little ladle they'd always put in their water that was neat. Then we'd take the butter we had made earlier, and we'd eat that butter on crackers. Homemade butter is real hard. It'd just crack the crackers up terribly if you weren't real careful. I cracked a lot of crackers, but it was such a special time together. I'd help make the butter, then I'd get to enjoy it.

"Today a lot of folks don't realize that it's the little things that make memories for kids. I wouldn't take a million bucks for mine."

In the afternoon, Gene Wilson and his school bus would stop in front of Grandma's house to pick up Susie and take her home. On most days the little girl couldn't wait to race inside and tell her mother all the things that had happened that day. With wide eyes she would repeat stories, talk about what they had eaten, and share what she had learned. To listen to her talk, one would have sworn that Susie thought she had been with the most important person in the world—and maybe she had.

As wonderful as the weekdays were, there were many weekends spent at Grandma's that were even more special. These were the times when the little girl got a chance to share even more intimate moments with the woman who was quickly becoming her role model.

"I remember when I'd get to spend the night with them." Susie's eyes lit up at the memory. "We would go to bed, and I could hear so many different things. They lived way out in the country, and I could hear the whip-poor-wills and the bobwhites singing all night. I'd also hear her praying every night. She was a Pentecostal woman. When she was praying, I couldn't understand what she was saying and I'd say, 'Grandma, what are you praying? What are you saying?' And she'd say, 'Well, honey, I'm just praying to the Lord.'

"She would always take us to church on Sunday too," Susie recalled. "A lot of the time I didn't want to go. I thought I didn't need church, that it was boring. So I'd say that I wanted to stay home. But I really didn't have a choice, and I would load up with them and go. And you know, when I got there I really enjoyed it because I'd hear her singing. Sometimes my grandpa and she would sing little duets. I can almost hear them now, their singing touched me that deeply.

"Now, looking back on it, just about everything Grandma did sowed a lot of good home seeds. She lived a Christ-centered life, and so the examples she set and the way she touched me have always stayed with me."

Reba Smith's influence didn't end when Susie started to school and quit coming over every day. It didn't end when the little girl grew up and began to do things on her own. It didn't end even when Reba was called home to meet her Savior. In reality, her influence was so strong and so deep that it couldn't end, no matter what happened.

When Susie grew up, she felt the call to touch lives just as her grandmother had. She wanted to share with those who had not had the experience of the Reba Smith faith. At first she sang in churches, then moved to concert stages. Then she discovered a group that had been overlooked by preachers and missionaries — the rodeo cowboys, the athletes who spent their life on the road, their days in the arenas, and their nights often in bars. No one was preaching to them, no one was sharing the love of Christ with these modern-day vagabonds.

What Susie and her husband, Paul, could not have known was that their early attempts to set up worship services for rodeo performers would become one of the building blocks for a new type of Christian outreach — cowboy churches. These churches were inspired by the work Susie helped start at rodeos through her Christian concerts and devotionals. In the late 1990s, tens of thousands came to know the Lord through these cowboy churches. But without the influence of her grandmother, Reba Smith, Susie probably never would have been led to do this work.

"Every time I sing in front of a crowd," Susie said, "even at this age, I can imagine Grandma smiling down on me from heaven. She is seeing the seeds that she so patiently sowed coming to fruition."

In 1992, Susie was singing in a church just west of Lubbock, Texas. She was there to perform for a group of men and women she didn't know, and she fully expected that this service would be the same as a thousand others. Then, as she looked out over the congregation, she spotted an old friend. In a center pew was a smiling face that belonged to the widow of Gene Wilson, the bus driver who so long ago had made it possible for her to go to Grandma Smith's house.

"When I saw her out there, I just stopped what I was doing and cried. I mean I just cried right in the middle of the service. Then I said, 'Well, Millie, what are you doing here?' I told all the people about Gene driving the school bus and taking me to my grandma's house. I told them what that had meant to my life. I told them that Gene was an instrument of the Lord, a part of who I am, the man who helped me get to know my grandmother in a really special way. I also told the folks that night that they had better slow down. Most of them were running by their lives without even bothering to take the time to see or experience any of it. The fact is that few of us take the time to reach out like Gene or share like Grandma."

The world has changed dramatically since Reba taught Susie. No longer do rural folks live in such great isolation. Few women today take the time to grow large gardens or make everything they use. Certainly four-year-old children don't hop on the local school bus to ride to their grandmother's house every day. Yet the examples that Reba Smith gave to Susie—the humble way she prayed, the simple and sincere way she lived each facet of her life—remain embedded in her granddaughter's soul. They are a part of the richness of her life and the reason her own ministry has led so many to the Lord and been so successful in reaching a segment of society long overlooked by mainstream churches.

Susie Luchsinger probably will never churn butter or gather eggs again, and she will never again draw a bucket from a well to sip a cool drink of water from a chipped ladle. But she has already faced some of the same spiritual problems she saw challenging her grandmother on a daily basis. Without the older woman's example, Susie would have met these problems unprepared, and she might have made vastly different choices. Without the influence of her mentor's words and actions, who knows if today Susie would be sharing her message of salvation across the country and around the world through her testimony and music. Who knows if Susie's sister Reba McEntire would have kept her perspective and faith as she rose to the top of the entertainment world. A grandmother's morality deeply impacted the way both women grew up and face life today. And through these two sisters, the world has been touched in a huge way.

In Susie's mind, the image of her grandmother is as alive today as it was when she sat churning butter on a porch swing three decades ago. In her heart, that still strong voice reaches out and comforts her daily. In her soul, the old woman's wisdom still grows.

"I remember so many things Grandma did that showed me the Christian walk. She didn't just talk the talk, she walked it. From my earliest experiences I would just see her pour out her love for me in so many different ways. Isn't it a shame that today so many grandmas don't have time to do that for their grandkids?

"Each day I live it becomes more clear how much it meant that my grandmother took the time to do so many very simple things with me. We didn't go to fancy places or do things that took money. Yet what we did do — the talks, the prayers, the songs, and the cups of hot cocoa — gave me more than anything else could have. She touched my heart, and she gave me something that is with me still. The way she touched me was slow and easy, and it made a deep and lasting impression on me.

"One day, I walked up behind her while she was hoeing the flowers and she accidentally hit me with the back end of her hoe. Yet even that was meaningful and special because she dropped everything and just hugged me and held me until I felt better.

"Today, kids' lives are so full of activities that they don't have the time to make memories. I'm so grateful that my life was slower and I have my memories. Those memories are so important."

In and around Boggy Creek, Oklahoma, folks still occasionally talk about Reba Smith's flower garden. Some of the old-timers say that nobody ever had a garden like she did. They say she could make just about anything grow. Nobody could ever remember a weed anywhere on her place, and there always seemed to be something blooming. And most of these same old-timers will agree that the most important seeds Reba Smith ever sowed didn't come up in her garden. The products of countless hours of love and attention are now blooming around the world, touching the lives of millions. Susie Luchsinger knows this is true. After all, she is one of her grandmother's most precious flowers.

In today's world, grandparents have a greater impact on children than at any other time in history. More grandparents than ever before are directly involved in helping to raise their grandchildren. The opportunities to share values, to direct lives, and to pass along lessons anchored in faith are there like never before. A legacy of faith is there for the taking if today's grandparents will take the time to share the important life lessons as did a little-known Oklahoma farm woman.

As seen countless times in history, those lessons of faith can help start a movement that will touch tens of thousands whose grandparents did not share that vital message with them. Just ask Susie Luchsinger or Reba McEntire.

14

LOTTIE MOON

Faith to Take a First Step

Lottie used her boundless energy to become one of the most influential missionaries of her time. Yet her incredible witness would have been lost if she had not waged a war to allow women to share the message of faith. Her battles helped bring peace to millions.

Christmas Eve 1912, just off the Japanese coast, deep within the bowels of a slow-moving American steamship, a frail woman, not much over four feet tall and weighing just fifty pounds, was resting in a small berth under the deck. At seventy-five, this missionary looked as though she was used up. The endless vitality and incredible energy that had once set her apart from all those around her in the Chinese mission field was now gone, replaced by a resolute understanding of what lay just ahead.

At first glance the ship's passenger appeared to be of Asian descent. Her dress, her quiet tones, and her overly polite manners indicated she was a native of China. Yet her pale skin and round eyes hinted at much different roots. Inside this tiny shell of a woman resided two different and distinctly different cultures, a rarity at the time. What brought these worlds together and bridged the huge canyon between East and West was something Christians call the Great Commission.

Charlotte Digges Moon was born on December 12, 1840, outside of Charlottesville, Virginia, in a large plantation home known as Viewmont. Her father was a wealthy gentleman farmer who owned more than fifty slaves and dabbled in various outside businesses. He would spoil his seven children with gifts of clothing and trips while hiring the best tutors to educate the Moons at the family mansion.

In a sense the Moons were a part of Southern aristocracy, a segment of society many considered American royalty. Charlotte's idyllic life would continue until 1852, when Mr. Moon died of a heart attack while on a Mississippi riverboat.

Anna Maria Moon, Lottie's mother, then took up the reins of family leadership. Determined to see production in every area of her life, the widow pushed her children as hard as she pushed the workers on the plantation. Anna Maria demanded excellence. Her oldest son, Thomas, lived up to her standard and became a doctor. Orianna, who was two years older than Lottie, also earned a medical degree. She was the first woman in Virginia to become a physician. Now it was Lottie's turn to produce, but the path she chose was much different than that of her older brother and sister.

When Lottie was fourteen, Anna Maria sent Lottie to the prestigious Albemarle Female Institute, a boarding school in Charlottesville. In the classroom Lottie would excel in foreign languages and composition; outside the hallowed halls of instruction she would reign at creating havoc. She quickly became known as a class clown and prankster and earned the reputation as the worst disciplined student who had ever attended the Baptist institution. Her pranks were so numerous that whenever something went wrong, the teachers always came to her room first. And there was just cause for their constant suspicions. At fifteen Lottie climbed a long rope up to the school's large bell and muffled its clapper with towels and sheets. Classes started late that day. On other occasions she so scared fellow students with inflated stories of class and religious requirements that many ran away and had to be forcibly brought back to the campus. In her worst act of rebellion, she refused to go to church. She even told students that her middle name was Devil. For several years she was a principal's worst nightmare. It is little wonder that many teachers and students spent hours in prayer for the defiant girl's soul. Yet in spite of the way she challenged all those around her, the vivacious and fun-loving Lottie probably was the most popular student on campus.

Claiming boredom, Lottie attended a revival service during her senior year. She halfheartedly listened as a noted preacher spoke of the need for young people to get involved in Christian service. On the way back to the dorm, she made fun of what the man had said, getting several giggles from those who usually clung to her every word. Yet long after her classmates had gone to sleep, Lottie sat alone in the darkness replaying the man's speech in her head. By dawn, the young skeptic had experienced a revelation, deciding it might be in her interest to take a deeper look at the Scriptures. A few weeks later, completely consumed by the words of Paul and other early missionaries, she began to openly speak out on faith. As they listened to Lottie, the school's staff and most of the students were in a state of shock. They could not have been more surprised if they had been transported back in time and witnessed firsthand the parting of the Red Sea. Most expected Lottie's transformation to be a passing phase, but two years later, when Lottie emerged as the school's most dynamic Christian leader, even the skeptics decided that the Devil she had once claimed as her middle name had been completely pushed out of the young woman's life.

Lottie had already finished her undergrad degree and was working on her master's when two of her male friends informed her they were giving their lives to foreign mission service. Congratulating them, Lottie expressed interest in following their lead. The school welcomed her enthusiasm, but politely informed her that just as women could not speak in church or hold the post of deacon, they also were not allowed to become missionaries. If she wanted to work in the foreign service fields, she should marry a missionary and support him as his wife. Disappointed, Lottie stayed in school, earning her master's degree, then returned home to live with her mother on the family's plantation.

The Civil War would turn the Moons' world upside down. Death and destruction were all around them, friends left for battles and never came back, slaves claimed their freedom and the fields went unworked. Finally, at the war's end, the estate was largely sold off to pay bills, leaving the family only the home. Lottie took a job as a teacher at the Danville Female Academy in Kentucky. For five years a majority of what she made was sent back to her mother in an attempt to hold on to their beloved Viewmont. When her mother became sick and died, Lottie and the rest of the Moon children gave up any semblance of their aristocratic roots and sold the family home.

With her energy and attractive features, men constantly tried to catch the eye of the school's best-looking teacher. Lottie was flattered by the attention, but told her friends that she had felt, since the night when she had chosen to follow Christ's path, that she needed to remain single in order to fulfill a course already charted for her in Christian work. For the moment that seemed to be simply giving money to support male foreign missionaries, yet as she tithed her income, she prayed for a much larger role in taking the gospel to the world.

In 1872, Lottie's younger sister, Eddie, received permission to go to China with another missionary couple. The letters she sent back to America stoked the fire already burning in Lottie's soul. Just as she had been a rebel who broke rules when in school, the small teacher decided it was time to push the envelope again. This time she had a mighty cause in mind. She was determined to convince the Baptist church that women could be effective missionaries. Armed with letters from missionaries complaining they were unable to reach Chinese women because tradition forbade men to teach females, Lottie pointed out it was time for the old rules to be changed. She wrote to church leaders explaining it was time for women "to minister to the poor and suffering, establish Sunday schools, sewing schools, night schools, mothers' meetings. Our Lord does not call on women to preach, or to pray in public, but no less does he say to them than to men, 'Go, work in my vineyard.' "

After more than a year of lobbying, her logical arguments and fiery passion, coupled with the failure of the male missionaries to reach the women of China, finally caused a change in rules. On July 7, 1873, the heads of the Baptist denomination appointed Charlotte Digges Moon as a missionary to Tengchow, China. This should have signaled the fulfillment of a long dream, but instead the assignment would bring only great frustration. Though she left thinking of herself as a recognized missionary, Lottie would soon discover that because she was a woman she would be denied certain opportunities.

Rather than spread the good news of salvation, Lottie was assigned to teach in a school. The real missionary work remained in the hands of men. The girls she taught were mainly from wealthy families and had no real interest in learning. Lottie soon saw herself as little more than a Christian nanny. Rather than allow the preconceived ideas of a woman's role in the church to hold her back, she obtained a tutor of her own. In her spare time she studied the language, the culture, and Chinese history. As she learned more about the nation and its people, she gained a deep respect for all aspects of Chinese life. She also began to grow alarmed that most missionaries seemed intent on not just converting these people to the Christian faith but also erasing everything that was Chinese from their lives. It appeared to Lottie that other missionaries felt it necessary to have new Chinese Christians dress and act like little Americans. In their minds conversion was not complete until this transformation took place. Lottie sensed this practice would ultimately destroy the work. Just as she had in school, she refused to conform and accept established thinking. While others in her group tried to westernize the Chinese, she adopted the dress, language, and manners of the locals.

In late 1874, when her sister grew very ill, Lottie returned to America. During her time at home she spoke to church groups of her experiences, ending each address by begging for a chance to reach out to the Chinese people with her own evangelical voice. She constantly pleaded for the restraints placed on her mission due to her sex to be lifted. She felt God's power in her heart and wanted to let it loose in the mission field.

She told one group, "Can we wonder at the mortal weariness and disgust, the sense of wasted powers, and the conviction that her life is a failure that comes over a woman when, instead of the ever-broadening activities that she had planned, she finds herself tied down to the petty work of teaching a few girls."

With that message Lottie conducted a campaign to give women missionaries an equal voice. She addressed any group that would listen to her and wrote articles for all the area's periodicals. She also lobbied the highest powers in the church. So convinced was she that God wanted to use her as a hands-on missionary to China and that her concept of becoming Chinese to reach the lost of this vast land would work that she challenged the most powerful men of the day to find somewhere in Scripture that denied her this right. For three long years she fought her battle through her speaking engagements and writing, but her voice was indeed a lonely one as few joined her chorus. Even when she went back to China in 1877, Lottie remained handcuffed by church rules that kept her from doing the real work of a called missionary.

For the next eight years Lottie taught children and made minor attempts at doing more direct one-on one witnessing in the streets of China. Finally, in 1885, she grew tired of waiting on denominational approval and, on her own, moved into the country's interior to actually preach in the area of P'ingtu. The only missionary in the region, she took on the duties that had been prescribed only to men. Her work was met with great success. People of all ages flocked to hear the American who dressed, ate, and spoke as they did. Without formal approval, Lottie was winning converts. As her flock grew, she wrote home of the successes and bombarded her mission board with requests for recruits, including single women. "I estimate," she wrote, "a single woman in China is worth two married men." While a few church leaders congratulated the woman and assured her they would pray for her work, they offered little in the way of help.

Not satisfied with the response of the male church leaders of her day, Lottie began to write pieces aimed at women for Christian magazines. These features trumpeted the fertile ground she had cultivated and begged for women to get involved in raising money to send more missionaries, especially women. In her writing she reminded her readers about how important women had been in Christ's life. She presented profiles of women from other nations doing great things in the name of the Lord.

One article, "Women's Work," was deemed so militant that it almost cost Lottie the support of the Baptist mission board. In the feature she pointed out that while men did not mind women doing a lion's share of the missionary fieldwork, most women were still relegated to second-class status in the church. She demanded this attitude be changed so that more single women would be encouraged to accept calls as foreign missionaries. Women could do the work, she pointed out; their only handicap was the men who tried to handcuff them.

Her thoughts on the subject of female Christian service created such great controversy that many wanted to stop all support to her missions. Rather than cave in to what she viewed as archaic thinking, she fired back a letter and actually raised the stakes. She wrote that unless women were recognized as full missionaries, with all the rights of men in the mission field, she would give up her work. She argued that millions more souls could be saved if women were allowed to fully join this fight. She ended her communication by vowing that she would come home and fight for rights in America if satisfactory action was not taken in this matter. Lottie had just fired the shot that started a revolution.

While those who railed against her "unchristian" attitude considered her offer, Lottie's challenges provoked thought and discussions in women's Bible studies and prayer meetings all across the South and Midwest. Something needed to be done, the women agreed. So while the men tried to come up with a way to appease the militant Miss Moon, the women formed an organization to support the work of missionaries of both sexes. Calling themselves the Women's Missionary Union, these pioneering women pushed the message of the Great Commission in structure meetings and set about raising money to fund the work they saw as vital to fulfilling Christ's challenge. Establishing an annual fund-raising effort to coincide with Christmas, the women, in their first year of work, provided more than $3,300 to mission projects in China and sent three new missionaries to help Lottie with her work. This effort did more than lay a concrete framework for efforts in China; it probably saved Lottie's mission.

By 1887, the missionary's spirit and strength had almost played out. She was tired of fighting the board for money and help. She was exhausted from her long hours of work. She was also lonely. She no longer had contact with anyone who spoke English. She had no one who could offer her any physical or spiritual support. The needs of the people around her were immense. Many were sick, almost all were poor, and most did not have enough food for a single meal a day. Overwhelmed, Lottie opened her own small home to them. She allowed them to sleep on her dirt floor and to eat whatever small stores she had in her cupboard. She gave her heart and soul to these people. She felt as if she was the only one who really cared about bringing Christ to China.

During this lonely period, as doubt crept into her mind, she wrote, "Mission life takes the strength and energy out of us before we know it. I am bored to death with living alone. I don't find my own society either agreeable or edifying." She was so down that when she received an offer to teach at Harvard, she considered giving up her life's work.

About that time the gift and support from the newly formed Women's Missionary Union arrived, and the head of the male-run Baptist mission board informed Lottie that she was a full partner in the work and that no longer would male missionaries be considered her superiors. Lottie thanked the board, but replied that single women missionaries in all missions should have an equal voice. She argued that if this was done, thousands of new missionaries would flood the fertile gospel fields.

Over the course of the next year, Lottie's forecast was proven right. In China the men who were sent by her mission board almost always failed to stay more than a few years, while the women stayed on and had much more dramatic success in converting the Chinese to Christ.

Though still a flashpoint of debate in many churches in America, Lottie Moon was now growing into a legend in China. While

American men often viewed her with distrust, the men of her adopted nation respected her as one of the bravest they had ever met. They had seen her sacrifice, seen the way she had reached out to the sick and the poor, and noted the way she had adopted their customs without sacrificing her own faith, and it moved thousands to follow her. While male missionaries could not reach women and had limited success with men, Lottie's impact knew no boundaries.

Over the next decade she expanded her missions inland, setting up gospel centers and churches in scores of new villages and cities. She oversaw numerous food and medical programs. Though barely over four feet tall, she now carried herself and her faith as if she were a giant. Her confidence in God had grown to the point where she simply had no fear. She would go anywhere, alone if need be, to do his work.

In one city, she watched as a mob rushed a newly established Christian church and demanded it be destroyed and its members beaten. While the men of the church huddled inside, Lottie walked over to face the angry mob. The tiny western woman, dressed in traditional Chinese garb, quieted the enraged mob and, in their own language, boldly stated, "If you attempt to destroy this church, you will have to kill me first. Jesus gave himself for us Christians. Now I am ready to die for him." Even as they continued to shout at her, Lottie stood firm, looking the men in the eye, almost daring them to strike her. Finally, one person suggested it was time to go home and the crowd dispersed. Within two years, the church she alone defended became the largest in that part of China and a rock for Christian work for decades to come.

Over the next twenty years it seemed nothing could stop Lottie. She worked through the Boxer Rebellion, witnessing to people on both sides of the war. In 1911, during China's revolution, the fighting was so intense the U.S. consul asked missionaries to leave the area. All did but Lottie. When American doctors and nurses deserted a local hospital in Hwanghsien, she darted through battle lines and directed the facility herself. When the staff returned, she headed back to her own mission. Though she was over seventy, the diminutive missionary still carried a great deal of weight. When she reached the front lines, generals from both sides agreed that allowing the "Baptist Saint" to get back to her mission was more important than the battle at hand. They declared a temporary truce so Lottie could get home safely. The news of the American missionary who stopped a Chinese civil war spread worldwide.

After the revolution, famine spread across China. Lottie had seen hunger before, but not on this scale. There simply was not enough food for even the upper class. From her home in P'ingtu, she did all she could to feed those who had nothing. She opened her house and used all the money she had to buy rice. And when that food ran out, she sold the few possessions she had to buy more. When locals who had extra food offered it to the American they so deeply admired, she took it not for herself, but to give to others she felt needed it much worse than she did.

Months later, another American missionary saw how frail Lottie had become and sent word for help. A nurse, Jessie Pettigrew, examined Lottie and found her to be literally starving to death. Though she fought to stay with her people, Baptist officials demanded the now-legendary missionary return to America to get proper medical care. She was too weak to fight the order. A nurse, Cynthia Miller, was assigned to watch over Lottie as she began her journey home.

As the trip began, Miller encouraged the missionary with stories of what she could do when she got back to the States. Lottie smiled and seemed to keep up with the conversation, but did not participate. For most of the trip from her home in China to Japan, she appeared lost in thought. On December 23, the day the ship arrived in Kobe, Miller asked her patient if she had any Christmas wishes. Lottie did not respond, but rather began to sing "Jesus Loves Me" in Chinese. When the missionary concluded her performance, she smiled, said a short prayer, and fell asleep.

The next morning, Christmas Eve, with a bit more color in her face and life in her eyes, Lottie looked around her cabin. As Miller approached her bed, the elderly woman raised her arms up toward the ceiling, her fists clenched tightly in what the nurse knew was a traditional Chinese greeting. She held her arms aloft for several moments, her face framing a sweet look of peace, then her hands dropped to her side, and at that moment the missionary truly did arrive home.

Today Lottie Moon's name is more famous than it was when she fought for women to have the chance to fully be accepted as trumpeters of the Great Commission. Thousands of missionaries have been so inspired by her story that they have followed Miss Moon to mission work. Millions now annually support her cause through Christmas offerings. More than $1.5 billion has been raised in her memory since her death. And Lottie's China has become a nation where more souls come to the Lord each day than in any other nation on earth. All this happened because a woman who once was not even allowed to speak in her own church had the courage to start a movement that allowed anyone to stand up and share the good news.

Charlotte Moon was born into a privileged element of society; she once doubted there even was a God; but when she came to know him she gave up everything she had to serve that Lord. As she often said, "How many there are ... who imagine that because Jesus paid it all, they need pay nothing, forgetting that the prime object of their salvation was that they should follow in the footsteps of Jesus Christ in bringing back a lost world to God." She lived those words and inspired others to follow in her tiny footsteps. Lottie Moon surely lit the way for all of us.

15

KAY YOW

Faith to Win

Kay had no plans to become a great coach. She had no plans to become a vocal Christian. The fact that she has used her career and faith in her battle with cancer has given countless people the strength to battle on during life's toughest times. In the world of sports, she has proven to be the biggest winner.

On March 20, 2007, the clock was ticking down in the important NCAA tournament game between Baylor University and North Carolina State. As two exhausted teams fought for a chance to continue their run in the women's tournament, each passing second held more importance. In the last minute of the game, as she watched her team struggle to hold on, North Carolina State's Coach Kay Yow was praying for overtime. She felt if they could just get to the extra period, then her Wolfpack players would find a way to secure a victory. Pulling herself slowly from her chair at the bench, the sixty-five-year-old woman waved her hands and pointed out a weak point in the Bear's defense. As Yow directed her team, the eyes of the thousands there, plus the national television audience, should have been on the court, but even in the high drama of the final moments of this important contest, scores of people never took their eyes off the coach.

Almost everyone watching the game on this late winter evening knew Kay Yow should not have been coaching. The fact was she shouldn't have had the energy to even stand, much less pace the sidelines. She was sick, probably dying, and few in her condition could have lifted themselves from bed. Yet she was there, dressed in her school colors and doing her job. How did she did do it? That was a question she had been asked many times in the last few weeks. As Yow patiently explained, what pushed her was faith, and faith alone. What strengthened her was God. She was simply doing her job, answering her call, and trying to make a Christian impact on the kids she coached. Though most felt the disease raging in her body was going to kill her, she somehow saw it as one of the most glorious opportunities ever given to her. This was her chance to show the world what a woman of faith could do!

Behind the bench, watching her every move, was a nurse. A doctor sat in the crowd trying to keep an eye on Yow as well. The breast cancer, which she had beaten on two other occasions, had come back that fall. This time it was ravaging several different areas of her body. The coach, who had once moved with the grace and quickness of a deer, now struggled to lift her arms. It had taken her almost an hour to eat a small bowl of oatmeal that morning. Pain was her constant companion and strength a long-forgotten ally. And just like in the game she was coaching, her own clock was running. She had won more than seven hundred hard-fought battles on the hardwood, but there probably were few opportunities left to add to that total. Still, she smiled and embraced even this painful moment as a blessing. While others lamented the bad breaks she had been given, Yow exclaimed again and again what a wonderful life it had been.

Forty-three years before that night, when Kay walked across the stage at East Carolina University, she became the first in her family to obtain a college diploma. Unlike her parents, whose lives had been spent in North Carolina textile mills, Kay was entering a world filled with opportunities. The dark-haired, slender twenty-two-year-old had chosen teaching as a positive way to impact lives. With a degree in hand, all she had to do was find a classroom to call home. She was confident, through the study of the words of Mark Twain and Elizabeth Browning, she would get to touch a few young lives.

A. Doyle Early had been an educator for three decades when Kay's job application crossed his desk. The principal of Allen Jay High School, which had an enrollment of just four hundred, rarely got excited by the resumes of recent college grads. But this young woman's caused him to leap up from behind his desk and race down the hall. Running into the superintendent's office he shouted, "This is the person we've been looking for! This young woman will change Allen Jay High forever!" Somehow, Early's enthusiasm was greeted with skepticism until the principal explained why Yow's application could mean so much to the school. Allen Jay was hungry for a winner, and in Kay, both men saw a chance to get one.

Less than a week later, the two men sat down with the nervous applicant. "You have what it takes to be a great teacher," Early assured Kay. "And you have something else we need: the ability to coach our girls' basketball team."

The shy young woman took a moment to fully comprehend what had been said. Then Early continued, "I remember when you played for Gibsonville High. You averaged thirty-four points a game! You were the best high school player I'd ever seen. If you'll coach for us, the English job is yours."

It took only a split second for Kay to file a protest. "But I'm an English major. I don't know how to coach. I didn't even play basketball in college."

Grinning, the principal assured her he had complete faith in her abilities, even if she didn't. "You know the fundamentals and you know how to win. That's what our kids need. You're a winner, Kay."

Yow did not agree to coach. She first visited with family and friends. Each person she talked to urged her to grab the opportunity. But she still had reservations. Ultimately it was not her self-confidence but others' faith in her abilities that led her to sign the contract. A few months later, after spending the summer and fall reading countless books and visiting with scores of coaches, Kay watched her players go through their initial paces on the hardwood floor. She sensed that for most of them, practice was something to be endured until the game. Kay needed for them to get over that mental hurdle, to understand that to become winners they had to leap into preparation with as much energy and joy as they did the game itself. This was the first hurdle in her coaching career. The way she addressed it set in motion a philosophy she would embrace for years to come.

Blowing her whistle, Coach Yow called her players to the sidelines. In a quiet but firm voice she said, "Each of you needs to realize just how vital every element of practice is. You have to do your best all the time. Every shot you take must be executed properly. Excellence is not a gift; it is achieved by preparation and hard work. You will play how you practice. I will work hard, and if each of you will do the same, we will achieve something we can be proud of."

Outworking the kids in order to inspire them to treat each day as if it were their last chance to prove themselves, Kay set in motion a standard that would spell success from her first game, a philosophy she was still preaching forty-three years later. The success of that philosophy had propelled her, as a college coach, into the Basketball Hall of Fame.

Four years after that first high school win, with four straight conference titles under her belt, Kay left Allen Jay High School to return to her high school alma mater. After a successful season there, she moved on to tiny Elon College. In four seasons her teams won eight out of every ten games. It now appeared that the faith A. Doyle Early had shown in her nine years before had been justified. To fully prove the principal correct would require a career move taking women's basketball to major colleges.

In 1975, North Carolina State University, located in Raleigh, began a search to hire a full-time women's basketball coach. The men's basketball team was already consistently ranked among the top teams in the nation. But the women's program had only recently been moved to the varsity level. The university wanted a coach with strong leadership skills as well as someone of great character. The president and athletic director felt Kay Yow had both. Yow took the job, but with great hesitation.

As Kay set foot on the large college campus, she felt deep doubts. "What have I gotten myself into?" Kay asked herself as she initially strolled across the grounds. For the first time since her rookie year in coaching, she wondered if she could do the job and was leaning toward believing she couldn't. Deep down she felt this was simply too great a challenge for a small town girl.

Kay was still organizing her office when a student named Laurie Moore approached her and asked if Yow and her players would attend a special meeting for their team. The local chapter of the Campus Crusade for Christ was hosting the event and hoped to have all the teams on campus attend. If the campus athletes showed the courage to stand up for Christ, the Crusade group thought regular students might follow that lead. Initially, Kay declined, citing other obligations, but Moore would not give up. Finally, after running out of excuses, Yow accepted. Three decades later, as the clock ticked down on the NCAA tournament game and maybe her life, she wondered what would have happened if she hadn't gone that fall night so long ago.

Twenty students gathered on that mid-1970s night. Soon after the opening prayer, and just minutes into the meeting, the already bored coach allowed her mind to drift to her "to do" list. Though it appeared as if she was paying attention, she remained unaware of the events around her as she planned out drills for her first practices. Her obliviousness almost caused her to miss a question that would dramatically change her life: "If you died now, would you go to heaven?"

As if awakened by a flash of blinding lightning and the crash of thunder, panic rumbled through Kay's body. It shook her insides like a major earthquake. She had never felt so much pressure, not even as a high school player who had to make a shot to win a game. She wondered, "Would I go to heaven?" She remained stuck on that frightening thought as the student continued, "What is Number One in your life?" "Basketball," Kay admitted. "That's my whole life and that's wrong."

As the girl ended her testimony, Kay thought, "I've been a good person, but I have never had a personal relationship with God." At that moment, with that realization, everything else for Kay took a backseat. Pulling within herself, Kay prayed a silent prayer for God to come into her heart and her life. By the time the meeting ended, the coach experienced a peacefulness she hadn't felt in years, and for the very first time she was assured that she wasn't alone. Kay now had a new goal in life: not only to coach but to share with others her Christian faith.

Until she invited the Lord into her life, Kay had looked at every challenge as something she had to face alone. Now she realized God would always be with her. It amazed her how much this knowledge strengthened her every move and brought confidence to each new decision. She had told her first team on her initial day of coaching that preparation was the key to meeting any challenge, and with that in mind, Kay began studying the Bible. She worked as hard on understanding her faith as she did practicing free throws and jump shots. She worked on Bible drills to sharpen her ability to discuss her faith with others. The coach also joined the Fellowship of Christian Athletes and became an active member of a local church. When she was confident she understood her faith and the rules that came with it, she looked for ways to teach others.

Kay was still a rookie coach at North Carolina State and a first-year believer when she began sharing her spiritual beliefs. At one of her first speaking engagements she told the young people who had gathered to hear her, "What makes a tree able to withstand storms isn't its size but its root system. By turning our lives over to God, and by praying and studying God's Word, we can develop a complex and strong personal root system to withstand life's storms.

"The same is true when we participate on a sports team," she added. "If we work hard and invest our minds, hearts, and spirits, we will be able to withstand the challenges of the game. We can become leaders not only on the court but at our schools and in the community."

At the time she spoke those words the coach was trying to make a point to a few young people. Little did she realize that years later it would be her living out her own words that would sustain her in the toughest battle of her life. For the moment, being a Christian was one of the easiest things she had ever attempted.

During the next fourteen years, Kay's teams won three Atlantic Coast Conference titles, a gold medal at the 1986 Goodwill Games in Moscow, and a world championship. As a coach and a Christian, Kay was a success in every way. In truth, it had been a cakewalk. Everything she touched seemed to be successful. For the bright woman, life had offered only very manageable challenges. Living on faith was one of the simplest exercises she could imagine.

It was as she prepared to coach the 1988 Olympic basketball team that living on faith became a much larger challenge. In mid-July, the year before the games and feeling on top of the world, the coach went in for a routine physical. Her doctor suggested that because of her age she have a mammogram. The test revealed something in her breast that looked suspicious. After performing a biopsy, her doctor delivered the bad news, "Kay, you have cancer."

As the doctor's words sank in, Kay thought, "I can't have cancer, I have too much to do." For Kay there were now two critical questions: Would she beat cancer? Would she be allowed to serve as the U.S. Olympic basketball coach? She knew the only thing to do was to turn it over to the Lord.

The biopsy, having proved the cells were malignant, led to Kay's decision to have a mastectomy. Following the operation, the doctors determined the disease had been caught early and gave her the go-ahead to make plans to coach for North Carolina State. But some people still questioned whether she had the needed stamina to lead the team so soon after surgery. The coach doubted it as well. One day when things looked bleakest, Kay prayed that God would grant her the strength to handle whatever happened. Finishing her prayer, she left her office and began a workout with her team. As the players gathered around their coach for the usual post-practice evaluation, Kay's heart swelled as she realized she was again physically able to do her job. Suddenly she felt great.

But as she studied her players' faces, she knew they were deeply concerned about her. For the coach it was like taking a step back in time, to that first day on the Allen Jay High School court. Smiling, she said, "There are many things in life we can't control, but we can always control our attitudes. With faith in God, we can face all challenges. We can find a way over, around, or through every obstacle."

A few weeks later she told another group, "Cancer may bring to light the brevity of life, but God has shown me that panic won't help and neither will self-pity. As I have battled cancer, God has been my focus, and I know that nothing is impossible with him." Then, with a smile on her face and tears in her eyes, Kay added, "I get so emotional sometimes, but these are tears of joy. You see, I am part of God's plan, and so are you. God uses pain to give us some of our greatest personal growth and triumphs. Without him, all victories, even over cancer, would be hollow. God gives life meaning and purpose."

After the meeting, an elderly woman also battling the disease grabbed Kay and, with tear-filled eyes, whispered, "You're right, I can make it." That woman was just the first of many with cancer that Kay would touch.

Yow spent the next year helping to raise hundreds of thousands of dollars as the honorary chairperson for the Lineberger Comprehensive Cancer Center in Chapel Hill. Just as her first coaching job was not something she had wanted, neither was cancer. But in both cases, she focused on the opportunities.

Proving she could coach the Wolfpack, Kay took up the reins of the Olympic team. In Seoul in September 1988, the American women won their first four games. Before the final game, against an older, more experienced team from Yugoslavia, Coach Yow gathered her players in the locker room. Studying the face of each of the women, Kay silently asked God for the right words to show that she had faith in them.

"You have worked hard for this opportunity," Kay began. "Today, you have the chance to prove you are the best. Work hard, hang tough, go the distance. In life, none of us know what that distance is. And while the distance isn't under our control, the way we play and the enthusiasm we show is under our control." When the final buzzer sounded, the scoreboard showed Kay and her team had notched another victory and claimed the gold medal.

Yow's battle with cancer was far from over. More than a decade later, the cancer came back. Though the fight was tougher this time, the disease was no match for the coach and her faith. Then in November 2006, she noted a loss of energy; even the easiest tasks wore her out. It would take a medical professional to officially give her the news, but Kay was sure that her old foe had come back for another round. Tests proved her right.

The first two times she dealt with cancer, Kay coached through it. This time the punches landed by the illness were too heavy for the coach to withstand. Within weeks, the cancer had floored her. She was almost too weak to brush her teeth. Every movement brought numbing pain. Even walking a few steps was a challenge. Her strong lungs, which had carried her through long games, now seemed to forget how to take in air. Finally admitting she was no match for this determined enemy, Kay turned over the coaching duties to an assistant. It broke her heart to stay away from the campus and the kids she loved.

Kay knew what the odds were. She had battled this villain twice before. Her success in those battles had become a lightning rod for raising money to provide new research for the fight against breast cancer. Yet she realized that it would be years before some medical miracle could address what was hitting her now. Though a stage IV demon was ravaging her body, and treatment was causing food to taste like metal and her hair to fall out while turning her hands and face as dark as brown leather, she still watched every game she could on television. It was during this time, when she was closer to death than life, that she began to see just how much her previous battles had accomplished. She was honored when one week of the NCAA season was set aside to call attention to breast cancer. She was overwhelmed when she noted that many were pointing to her courage and faith as the reason for the spotlight being placed on the fight against the disease.

In a nationally televised game from Norman, Oklahoma, a showdown between rival Texas and Oklahoma, every one of the more than eleven thousand fans in the arena wore a pink breast cancer awareness T-shirt. The two teams replaced their regular shoestrings with pink ones, and OU's Coach Sherry Coale, known for stylish high heels, wore pink sneakers with her stylish dress suit. In various ways this scene was repeated on campuses from coast to coast. Because of that one week, millions of dollars were raised for cancer research. And the coaches interviewed after the games almost always talked about Kay Yow. Hundreds called her the finest Christian they had ever known.

Tumors may have been trying to strangle every part of her body and she might have found it hard to walk more than a block at a time, but seeing the kind of support she was getting from those in her profession caused Yow to walk back into the gym. Her team had been suffering without her, but with the coach now directing practice and leading them into games, things dramatically changed. Suddenly a team that appeared destined to finish in the bottom half of the league standings reeled off ten victories in a dozen games, beating the teams ranked number one and number two in the nation on consecutive nights. In the midst of this incredible run, Kay won her seven hundredth game and her team made the NCAA tournament. Yow, who had seemed at death's door a few weeks before, was now at the heart of one of the most remarkable turnarounds in basketball history.

Now it was March 20 and she was battling former National Champion Baylor Lady Bears. The day of the game many felt Yow would not be able to coach. The disease had spread to her skeleton and liver. All indications were that her time on earth was to be measured in weeks or less. Kay spent part of that trying week attending to her father, who died of heart failure at the age of eighty-seven. As a long list of demands rained down on her, she found herself having breathing problems. She woke up the morning of the game to discover her fingernails literally falling off her hands. Her blood pressure was high and her heart was racing. The chemicals used to treat the invading disease probably were causing as many problems as the cancer. Just a few days before, she collapsed during a practice. Her stunned players had watched as she was whisked to the hospital in an ambulance. It seemed obvious to everyone but Kay that her body was sending up the white flag. Yet even as they wheeled her to the vehicle, she had been yelling out things for the team to work on during the remainder of practice.

"She took a chance that further inspiration by her might spur this group of women to do something they didn't even think they could do," a close friend explained.

Yet the players told the press that it was not the actual coaching that pushed them on, it was Coach Yow's faith. "She gives us incredible energy and inspiration," explained Danielle Wilhelm, a senior guard. "She never stops fighting, so we can't stop fighting."

"That's how Coach Yow is as a person," added Ashley Key. "With everything she's going through, she's still smiling. She's still having fun. Players want to take that on the court with them."

To make it to the game against Baylor, Yow had to consume large doses of medication for her nausea, receive several bottles of intravenous fluids, and force herself to eat a bit of a chicken sandwich. Still, she could barely walk to the car. She knew, just as Principal A. Doyle Early had told her so many years before, coaching was her calling. Because of taking that first job, she had been able to touch so many lives over the past four decades. So many had come to know the Lord through her example and so many had fought cancer with her, standing as a testament to their faith. Now she could feel those people urging her on. With every step she took, the pain subsided. When she made it onto the court, the energy had returned, the pain was gone, and she felt God all around her. For the moment, cancer was being driven away by faith.

As the game started, those who knew her well, including many on press row and hundreds of fans in the stands, had tears in their eyes. The announcers at ESPN as well as fans from coast to coast were trying to understand how this woman could crawl out of bed, much less coach. If they had been at a recent awards dinner and heard her speak, they would have understood. Standing proudly, she told the audience that night, "God has blessed me a hundredfold more than anything I could face in this life. God is my anchor.

"For me, my faith [in God] is everything in getting me through this. In Psalms there is a passage that says, 'The Lord is the sustainer of my life.' I believe what he says. There is another great verse in Psalms that says, 'You have cloaked me with strength for battle.' And my favorite verse is in Philippians, 'I can do all things through Christ who strengthens me.'

"There are many things in life we can't control . . . but with faith in God, we can face all challenges. God uses pain to give us some of our greatest personal growth and triumphs . . . and gives life meaning and purpose. He is the head coach. He has a game plan for my life and for yours."

North Carolina State got the extra time they needed on that March night. They took Baylor to overtime and beat the Bears 78-72. The victory kept Kay Yow smiling and seemed to buy the coach a bit more time as well. A week later, against one of the nation's best teams, the University of Connecticut, the dream season ended. At the conclusion of the game, an exhausted Yow spoke of taking a couple days off, then beginning to work with her freshmen, preparing them for the next season. What she really was doing was providing them with a model for faith-based living that they could use for the rest of their lives.

"This season," Associate Head Coach Stephanie Glance told the media, "will be etched in our memories forever. We learned about what a group of people can do under adverse circumstances. Coach Yow is battling for her life. She's taught the players so much about life, and then they get to see her living it out. It's a wonderful gift."

It was the faith of a man she did not know that pushed Kay Yow into a profession where she not only changed the game of basketball but where her own faith shaped the lives of countless players, coaches, fans, and thousands of others who have no idea how to dribble a ball. It was faith that carried her through three battles with cancer, and those battles led to millions of dollars being raised to help new generations of women suffering from this disease. It was faith that inspired thousands to fight when they thought they had no fight left in them.

And it was faith that brought her back to the court when she was too weak to coach by herself. Yet, as she proved in that two-month run, when God is with you, you are strong enough to do anything.

For two decades Kay Yow used a dreaded disease as a way to present her faith to the world. Cancer became a platform, and many who came to know Yow also came to know the object of her strength. Even as the clock wound down on what might be her last game as a coach, she kept fighting.

"The truth is," she explained to the readers of *USA Today*, "I could be taking some level of chemo and drugs forever, unless the Lord gives me a miracle. Which, by the way, I don't count out." And as Kay knows, you can't count out anyone who has faith.

16

SOPHIE SCHOLL

Faith to Challenge Evil

When the adults around her hid their faith and convictions, this young girl leaned on her faith and stood up to Nazi Germany. Sophie paid the ultimate price, but in doing so she continues to inspire young people around the globe today.

On February 22, 1943, Sophia Magdalena Scholl sat by herself at a small table in a dank, dark prison cell. She hurriedly dashed off three letters, writing as if death itself were chasing her. And in truth, for this college student, the clock was ticking much faster than it was for her peers. Sophie, as her family called her, was less than two months short of her twenty-second birthday, and though the attractive brown-eyed brunette was not physically ill, she was nevertheless dying. In her case the cause of death would be courage. Sophie had lived much of her life on faith and now would die because of it.

There were more than fifty million people living in Germany as Sophie waited alone for her executioner. By this time, as a world war initiated by their own leader raged around the globe, millions in this European nation were aware of the demonic nature of the Third Reich. Still, when decisions of their government flew in the face of everything they believed and held dear, they did not challenge authority. Even most leaders of the church in Germany turned a blind eye to what Hitler was doing. With the moral authorities of the era remaining silent, Sophie came forward to publicly proclaim that God's people could no longer support evil incarnate masked as blind patriotism. In a peaceful, nonviolent campaign of words, she and a small group of friends challenged the youth of Germany to stand up with one voice and demand change in the nation. Though she never picked up a gun, her actions made her the Nazis' public enemy No. 1.

It shouldn't have turned out like this. Sophie was bright, friendly, charismatic, and talented. She should have been recognized as one of her nation's most gifted. Sometimes, embracing faith calls for sacrifice, and no one in Germany was more ready to give up her own life and all its promise than was this diminutive student.

Sophie was born in Forchtenberg on the River Kocher, the fourth of five children. Her father was a business manager who moved to consulting work about the same time as Sophie entered grade school. Though he would later become mayor of Ulm, his daughter seemed to have little interest in politics. While Hitler rose to power, the girl studied art, reading, and music. At age twelve she even joined the League of German Girls, a Nazi youth organization that, on the surface, resembled the Girl Scouts. Sophie and her friends, however, would soon discover the league was much more interested in fostering propaganda and devotion to the führer than in developing camping and cooking skills. In the meetings God was de-emphasized and Hitler was lionized. Yet even though the league's agenda went against her Christian faith, it was not until 1937 that Sophie began to understand the threat slowly strangling her nation and her family's deep Christian heritage.

Sophie's older brother Hans had joined an organization known as the German Youth Movement. Though it had been fostering leadership skills in young men for more than four decades, the führer saw the group as a rival to his own Hitler Youth. In truth, many facets of German Youth were diametrically opposed to what the National Socialist Party embraced. At campouts and meetings, German Youth instructors would present the negative points of Hitler's movement. In 1937, Hans and several others from his troop were arrested for expressing ideas that railed against the views of the government. Though they were not held long, local authorities demanded that each of the boys recognize the divine appointment of the nation's leader and then pledge to live and die for Hitler. This action clearly spelled out that any type of dissent would lead to harsh punishment. As the dictator put the last elements of his power together, opposition became mute.

Sophie was deeply affected by her brother's arrest and the warnings that went with his release. As she looked into her community, read newspapers, and listened to radio, she began to realize that freedoms she took for granted were being erased in the name of progress and loyalty to the fatherland. She could not understand why others were not appalled at what to her seemed obvious. The man who owned the house where they lived was Jewish. Suddenly, because the Nazi movement preached that Jews were the cause of most of Germany's problems, he was forced to give up his property and was quietly removed from their city. Others disappeared as well. Books she had once openly read were burned. Her father had even been told to hold his tongue in public forums. Free speech was reserved for those who mirrored the state's message.

For the teenager, the lessons she learned in her Bible seemed to be out of touch with those she witnessed in the new order. The morality she embraced as a Christian had been affected as well. More and more it appeared that Hitler was replacing God in Germany. In some churches the name of the führer was spoken more than the name of Jesus. For Sophie to finally find the faith she needed to stand up and challenge the madness, she would have to be exposed to the real horrors of Nazi rule.

Much more than any of her friends, Sophie was a deep thinker. This was especially true when it came to her theology. A voracious reader, she studied Bible commentaries more than many pastors. Over time she developed a philosophy that mirrored that of Augustine. Like her spiritual role model, she wrote down all her sins, even the smallest ones, and tried to eliminate them from her life. She constantly battled to push any evil from her own nature. In time she would apply this standard to the actions of her nation.

When Sophie graduated from high school, war was raging and German tanks were rolling across eastern Europe at will. The nation was in high spirits, buoyed by a sense of invincibility created by a host of dynamic military victories. Hitler was universally praised in the press, on streets, and from pulpits. The nineteen-year-old high school graduate was required by German law to spend a part of 1941 in the auxiliary war service. There she first began to hear the horrid war stories and the ramifications of the "Final Solution." The knowledge of these things, ignored by most of the country, would eventually lead Sophie to take part in a passive political resistance movement.

Her first awakening came when one of her former teachers, a man she loved for his wit, charm, and grace, was taken from the school. In Sophie's hometown, the honorable man was pushed out into the street, knocked to the ground, and held down as first soldiers and then students spit on him. He was beaten and loaded onto a train bound for Poland. His only crime was being Jewish.

Sophie next learned of students whose "social" problems had caused them to be quietly taken from their families and transferred to government facilities. The parents were told the students were going to a much better place where they could receive the tools necessary to live a productive and happy life. Many of those who boarded the trucks were retarded. Their destination was not another school, but a gas chamber. They were being exterminated like pests. The sweet voices of these victims, happily singing as they were taken away to what they thought was an exciting, wonderful home, haunted Sophie's nights. After the developmentally disabled were removed, the trucks came back for the insane and the elderly. None of these victims ever returned home.

Because of her good looks and sense of style, Sophie had her share of boyfriends. One of them, Fritz Hartnagel, had fought with soldiers who had been on the Eastern Front. When Fritz returned home, he shared two stories that moved Sophie to tears. In Poland and Russia, when the soldiers had overrun villages, Jews and ethnic people had been rounded up and forced to dig large pits. Then, when they had completed their work, they were tossed into the pits and shot. Their age or sex made no difference; even children were murdered.

Fritz knew the rumors of death camps were true as well. The Jews, such as Sophie's former teacher who had been put on a train for relocation, were being killed like animals. Hartnagel painted a bleak picture of the conditions in which these men, women, and children lived, and the chambers where they died and the ovens where their bodies were disposed of.

At first Sophie was embarrassed that these practices had the government's seal of approval. Then she became angry that the men who wore German uniforms were not just allowing this to happen but were participating and finding ways to rationalize their behavior as "just following orders." Finally, when the full weight of the millions who had already been murdered took root in her heart, she grew incredibly sad. It seemed her nation was intent on wiping out the very people Christ spoke of in Matthew 25:35–40. If Hitler had his way, "the least of these" would be eliminated from the world.

Sophie saw the actions of Germany as sinful. She found the inaction of those who chose to ignore these acts as an affront to the Christian faith. Where were the voices of reason? Where were the men of God who should be shouting this news from the pulpits? Where was the soul of the nation she had always thought of as being Christian in compassion and action? As she told her friend, "I have sympathy for the oppressed. I cannot just stand by and watch. How I look forward to paradise where such creatures cannot be killed."

For months Sophie internalized her sense of moral outrage. She prayed, studied her Bible, and sought a way to rationalize her hatred of Hitler and his henchmen along the biblical message of forgiveness and love. Still, as a lone voice, she sensed she could do little. As she prepared to enter the University of Munich in May 1942, she began to share her convictions and concerns with her brother.

Hans had already banded together with a few other students who loved hiking, sports, and philosophy. The group appeared innocuous, but in the safety of the wilderness, where the secret police could not overhear their conversations, their talks of art and music turned to morality and politics. They became more convinced the Americans and British would soon overpower the Nazi war machine, and they discussed ways to overthrow Hitler and save their beloved nation. It would be a minister's sermon that provided them with a vehicle for their mission.

One of the group members had a pamphlet containing the story of 300,000 Jews who had been gassed in a concentration camp. Though the government had quickly confiscated a large number of the flyers, enough were distributed to open a few eyes to the Nazis' extreme methods. Hans sensed that he could secretly distribute information in the same way. Over time he believed that the real news of Hitler's methods would create enough outrage to lead people to revolt against the Third Reich. It was an excited Hans who shared his vision with his sister. Sophie, who had been praying for a way to help end the madness, immediately joined the students. Through this group, she believed she could fight for change and reason without compromising her faith.

Hans Scholl picked the group's code name from a Spanish novel about peasant exploitation in Mexico. Written in 1931, *The White Rose* covered the struggle of the lower class against the ruling class. The rose symbolized purity and beauty. For Sophie the name represented her view of Christ and his life on earth. Hans, his sister, and several others joined the underground movement. Like Hans and Sophie, Alex Schomorell, Willi Graf, and Christoph Probst were students dedicated to inspiring a revolution that would overthrow Hitler and his government. A philosophy professor, Kurt Huber, became their mentor.

In June the group wrote and distributed what would be the first of their six leaflets begging Germans to band together and rise up en masse against the Third Reich. As would each of the pamphlets that followed, the first quoted well-known historians and the Bible as it outlined various crimes committed by the German High Command. The writings were sent out via the mail and covertly dropped in high traffic areas in Munich and other southern cities. The group's point of view was made clear with messages like the following: "It is certain that today every honest German is ashamed of his government and who among us has any conception of the dimensions of shame that will befall us and our children when one day the veil has fallen from our eyes and the most horrible of crimes reach the light of day?" With biblical teachings obviously guiding them, it was also easy to see whom they were trying to reach. It was not surprising that the Gestapo urgently tried to identify the members of the White Rose. What was amazing was that in spite of an intense investigation, the group managed to hide in the shadows for eight months.

The message that came through in each of the flyers was that people needed to recognize the demonic nature of their own leaders and fully support the resistance movement against Hitler. Christians needed to stand up in such numbers as to prohibit their voices from being silenced. The White Rose argued that Germans needed to save the world for not only their own sakes but because God was calling them to do so.

By early 1943, the group was doing more than printing and distributing their flyers. Under the cover of darkness they were painting slogans on Nazi buildings. Thousands were waking up to graffiti reading "Down with Hitler" and "Freedom!" Written in tar, the group's work took hours to remove. With the White Rose message now read by thousands, the Gestapo redoubled efforts to find those behind the writings.

February 1943 began with German armies suffering a stinging defeat at Stalingrad, in Russia. Those in the White Rose saw this as key to their campaign. They sensed the loss would cause millions to find the courage to overthrow "the most contemptible tyrant our people have ever endured." And that was the tone of the sixth flyer printed on the night of February 17. Before class the next morning, Hans and Sophie dropped stacks of the White Rose flyer along the empty corridors of Munich University. Sophie pitched the final ones from a balcony. A janitor saw her toss the last few leaflets and called police. A few minutes later the Scholls were picked up and taken into Gestapo custody.

Sophie and Hans were separated and questioned for hours by the secret police. Investigator Robert Mohr was assigned to obtain the young woman's confession. He quickly found the student to be wise beyond her years. In an attempt to protect her brother and friends, she denied everything. Only when she learned her brother had been broken did she speak of her participation in the White Rose. But even then she would not give her confederates away. "My brother and I worked alone," she told Mohr again and again.

Mohr used several different tactics on Sophie. He tried being friendly, then cold, and finally hostile, but the young woman never broke. When she proclaimed she stood for decency, morality, and God, he yelled back at her, "God does not exist!" He hammered at Sophie, telling her that her words and actions had caused the defeat in Germany and how she was responsible for troops dying. He screamed that it was her responsibility to support her government at all times. After hours of verbal assaults, the unflustered woman calmly answered that a patriot speaks for good, not evil. Germany, under Hitler, she argued, was evil. She finally told Mohr, "I still believe that I acted in the best interests of my people. I would do it again. I will accept the consequences."

An exasperated Mohr sighed, "Do you know what will happen to you? You could be found guilty of treason and be executed."

Sophie nodded that she understood, and then calmly asked, "Will I be hanged or beheaded?"

Sensing there was no way to break her, Mohr literally washed his hands. He then handed Sophie a confession to sign and date.

Taken to her cell, the young woman spent the next three days reading the Bible and praying. She assured the guards that God was with her and she never doubted she was doing his work. She told her Russian cell mate that she had no regrets other than the pain her loss would cause her family. Sophie then added, "Should we stand here at the end of the war with empty hands when they ask the question, 'What did you do?' and we must answer 'Nothing.'" As she explained why she had to act, the Nazi prison staff wondered if Sophie was speaking of a coming judgment day for all those who allowed Nazi rule to overrun their own sense of morality or of the final reckoning before God.

When one guard asked why she took such a great risk, Sophie smiled and explained, "I want to share the suffering of those days. Sympathy becomes hollow if one feels no pain."

The show trial that the Nazis staged took place on February 22. Sophie's and Hans's lawyers were working for the state and offered no defense. Roland Freisler, Hitler's hanging judge, was brought in from Berlin to make sure justice was served. He questioned the Scholls and one other member of the White Rose, Christoph Probst. Freisler damned them in his opening statement.

Though the two male defendants seemed nervous and frightened by the judge's bombastic style, Sophie appeared relaxed despite facing a charge of high treason. The courtroom was circled with Nazi flags. Even with the judge screaming at her, "Look what the state has done for you," "Look what the führer has done for you," she remained calm. She knew she had no chance at any verdict but guilty. But she was convinced the publicity created by the trial would do more to spread the message of the White Rose than a thousand flyers. She honestly believed the proceedings would cause millions to see the real evil that was part of Nazi Germany. In her mind God had given her this platform to defeat Hitler, and she was going to use it to accomplish that end. Sophie would prove that the meek would truly inherit the earth, and that evil, no matter how strong, could not triumph over those who embrace faith.

When the judge demanded to know why she joined the White Rose, Sophie proclaimed in a strong voice, "Somebody, after all, had to make a start. What we wrote and said is also believed by many others. They just don't dare express themselves as we did. We fight with words to open people's eyes. The German people want God, not Hitler."

After only a few hours, Freisler pronounced the trio's fate. The court found them guilty, and each would be executed. Over the noise of those agreeing with the sentence and punishment, Sophie firmly announced, "You will be standing where we are standing now."

Returned to her cell, the convicted woman expected to live for another ninety-nine days. That was the legally mandated time between conviction and execution, and she hoped that during this period the Allies would overrun Germany and save her from the gallows. When the prison matron told her she had only three hours, the young woman was shocked. The matron noted that when Sophie looked out the window at the sunshine, a sense of peace flooded the room. God was still with her, surrounding her even in prison. Moving to a table, Sophie sat down to write a few letters to her loved ones. She had just finished when the matron came and took her to a holding room. Her parents were waiting for her there.

After hugging them, Sophie said, "Please don't worry about me."

Her father replied, "I am proud of you. You did the right thing."

Sophie's mother, speaking through tears, sighed, "You will never come through our door again."

Taking the old woman's hand, Sophie smiled and said, "We will meet in eternity."

Her mother answered, "Don't forget, Sophie, Jesus saves."

Sophie shook her head and asked her mother to lean on Jesus as well. She was then taken back to her cell.

A few minutes later Sophie prayed with the Stadelheim Prison minister. As she prepared for death, Sophie prayed that others would seek God and she asked for his blessing on all those around her, even the prison guards. Her final words were not for herself, but for the transformation of the world into a peaceful place.

After the prayer, two guards escorted her to the execution chamber. She was so calm it frightened the hardened men. As she made her final steps, she proclaimed, "The sun is still shining." The men knew it was her statement of faith that God was still with her and she was still strong. A few seconds later, at five o'clock, the guillotine's blade dropped and Sophie was beheaded.

A single copy of the sixth leaflet, the one that had cost Sophie and the rest of the White Rose their lives, was smuggled out of Germany through Scandinavia to England. The British and Americans reprinted it and, in the summer of 1943, dropped millions of copies of the flyer over German-occupied territory. Now called "The Manifesto of the Students of Munich," the leaflet that Sophie had died for inspired countless once-frightened men and women to join the resistance movement. Just as she had believed, the show trial brought to light the real horrors of the Nazi war machine.

In the almost seven decades since her death, countless schools and parks have been named after Sophie. Numerous books have been written about her life and a movie, *Sophie Scholl—The Final Days*, recently played worldwide spotlighting her exploits. A recent poll found her ranked as one of the ten greatest Germans of all time. Sophie placed ahead of Bach, Bismarck, and Einstein. One German magazine labeled her the greatest woman of the twentieth century. There is even an American group that honors victims of every holocaust, from World War II to Darfur, under the name the White Rose Society.

Faith caused Sophie to get involved, faith caused her not to give up her friends, faith gave her the strength to stand up to the hanging judge, and faith sustained her as she walked to her death. Her spirit lives because Sophie Scholl had an unwavering faith so strong it helped to bring the greatest evil the world has ever known to its knees.

MARILYN MEBERG

Faith to Recognize God's Sovereignty

The belief in God's sovereignty frees me to accept everything I have ever or will ever experience. Knowing all things are according to His will means I don't second-guess anything. I simply say, "Lord, let me rest in this experience even though I may not want it."

—Marilyn Meberg

She lost a child and a husband to death, but thanks to the lessons of her parents, as well as a strange childhood pet, Marilyn has not just endured but has inspired. One of the funniest women on the planet, she is also one of the deepest. Millions of women have discovered their faith through this one woman's words and example.

Marilyn Meberg could justly be called the "Prime Minister of Humor" for the dynamic Women of Faith organization. She has no doubt earned the title. Thirty weeks a year she leaves audiences rolling in the aisle with side-splitting humor based on deeply personal experiences. Marilyn's ability to seemingly touch the hearts of all who listen while also tickling their funny bones in speeches and through her books makes her one of the world's most gifted speakers and authors. Millions have been blessed by her insights, lifted by her thoughts, and brought to the Lord through her words, yet the world might never have come to know this charismatic Christian leader if it had not been for a turtle named Leroy Walker.

Marilyn was an only child, a product of the post–World War II years, the daughter of a Methodist minister and his schoolteacher wife.

Her mother, Elizabeth, was a serious, focused woman whose faith was as deep as the ocean. A praying dynamo, Elizabeth supported the work of her husband, Jasper, with a steadfast conviction that indicated she felt a call for Christian service as deep as was his.

Jasper, on the other hand, was a man who often seemed serious only about his work. His wacky sense of humor and quick smile drew people to him. In equal doses he dealt out spiritual guidance and humor, often at the same time. His unique way of looking at life allowed him to see rainbows around every bend and great joy in the everyday routine of life. From the time his daughter could speak, the Reverend Ricker found a soul mate. The two constantly worked to make everyone around them laugh.

Seemingly born with a drive to find a smile in every situation, it hardly seems unusual that Marilyn gravitated toward an uncommon kind of pet. At age five, when most children were adopting stray kittens or lost puppies, the bright-eyed preacher's kid was asking if she could keep a wandering turtle—or tortoise, to be more precise. Her mother had no problem with her daughter's choice of pets or even the name, Leroy Walker, as long as the turtle stayed outdoors. Yet, being outside, in what should have been a natural environment, would prove to be Leroy Walker's undoing.

Leroy had a taste for homegrown produce, which meant he was naturally drawn to the neighbor's vegetable garden. It didn't take long for his exploits to be noted. When caught in the act, rather than face immediate punishment, Leroy sped off at his top speed. Not surprisingly, he was apprehended. This led to Leroy Walker being placed under house arrest at the parsonage.

Marilyn did not see the convicted criminal as a hopeless case. In fact she felt her turtle could still become a productive member of society if he could simply learn to adapt to society's rules. In a move that had likely never been attempted, the bright, energetic five-year-old decided to leash-train Leroy. Getting the leash around the dawdling creature's neck was not much of a problem, but that is where the success of Marilyn's instruction ended. Rather than walk on command,

Leroy would simply pull his head into his shell. The preschooler discovered that her pet had no desire to listen to anything she said. He refused to learn. It seemed all he wanted was to be a turtle and do what turtles had done for thousands of years. If Leroy Walker could not have that life, then he would opt to exist inside his shell, and no amount of pleading was ever going to get him to come out.

Over the course of the next few weeks, Leroy grew more sluggish. Having been denied the garden he loved, he showed little interest in living. One morning, when Marilyn went out to check on her best friend, she found him dead. The little girl was crushed.

Marilyn's mother, sensing that Leroy Walker had come to mean a great deal to her daughter, decided to use the turtle's departure as an opportunity to spend some quality time with her child. She listened as Marilyn shared all of the dreams she had had for Leroy and how empty her life would be without her pet. As Elizabeth solemnly absorbed her daughter's thoughts, she began to explain how much God loved Marilyn. She spoke of Jesus, his birth and his resurrection and what that could mean in everyone's life. At that moment, death was very real to Marilyn—her heart and mind were very open to what dying meant—thus the girl was ready to hear about Christ paving the way to a life beyond the one on earth. By the end of the mother-daughter conversation and the prayer that followed, Marilyn had asked Jesus to come into her heart. Though she still missed Leroy Walker, the soon-to-be first grader now felt much better about her own life and God's place in it.

It was easy for Marilyn to observe Christ's impact on people's lives. As a preacher's kid she was literally surrounded by Christians. Yet some of the Christian attitudes she witnessed created more concerns than comfort, especially the old fogies at church whose standard answer for every problem was, "Must have happened because there is sin in his or her life." If someone grew sick, many couldn't keep themselves from saying, "Must be sin in their life." If someone lost a job, they offered that same counsel. As an elementary school student, the thought that every problem was caused only because people were not living right with God was a hard concept for Marilyn to deal with. That meant that when she dropped her communion glass during a service, causing everyone to glance her way, God must have caused it because "there was sin in her life." The guilt that visited the child all but caused her to run from any negative influence in her church and pull into a Leroy Walker–type shell. Fortunately, the "must have been sin in her life" crowd was not the primary influence in her life. If it had been, Marilyn probably never would have spoken at a single Women of Faith conference.

"My dad was a pastor of small rural churches in Washington," Marilyn explained. "My mom taught high school English, Spanish, and French. Mom was fun loving, but reserved and quiet. Dad was an extrovert, fun loving and exuberant. It was an interesting combination of personalities. They met at Nyack Seminary in New York. From the beginning of their relationship they committed themselves to a ministry of meeting people's needs.

"I was an only child. I wanted to bring a fun loving, lighthearted joy to Mother, who was serious and sometimes melancholy. Dad brought out the clown in me. He and I did a lot of laughing to cheer Mom up. I now think she had a lot of depression, but in spite of that persevered and did good things."

Keeping up with Marilyn was a huge challenge for her parents. She was a constant whirl of motion. She loved sports, even winning a spot on the high school tennis team, was an avid reader, and landed a part in every play during her four years in high school in Vancouver. But most of all, she was a social being. She had a large number of friends and loved to talk. Her ability to interact with people of all ages made her popular with everyone except the "must have been sin in her life" crowd. These frowning folks were simply mystified by the girl's ability to smile and laugh through everything. They must have thought sin caused that as well.

"Even as a young person," Marilyn laughed as she looked back over her life, "the game was being set. God knew all along the various bents he was putting in my psyche and my preferences. He knew that someday those would be pulled together in the very call that I felt I have had and continue to have."

When she graduated from high school, Marilyn had no set goal of impacting millions with her wit, charm, and faith. What she really wanted to do was study the human mind and try to understand how it worked. Thus she plunged headlong into a psychology major at Seattle Pacific University. She tackled her studies with all the energy she had once put forth trying to leash-train Leroy Walker. The only thing that caused her to detour from that course was a handsome older student. As she would find out someday, Ken, just like Leroy Walker, was in God's plan for her life too.

Ken Meberg was Marilyn's perfect match. He loved to laugh as much as she did. He was constantly looking for the good in people, and his personality and charm made him a human magnet. People gravitated to him and he in turn made their days brighter.

"I was in choir my sophomore year, and he was choir president," Marilyn recalled. After she met Ken, she put in motion a plan to get closer to him. This led to long discussions, interesting dates, and eventually an engagement. As Ken wanted to continue in graduate school, Marilyn switched her major to English so she could support them as he obtained his master's.

Ken would become the youngest school superintendent in California when he joined his wife in an education career. His success would allow Marilyn to give up her job when their son Jeff was born. As a wife and mother, Marilyn's life was idyllic. Over the next decade she had the time to not only tend to her son's needs but to go back to school and pick up a master's degree in English. When she became pregnant for the second time, it seemed that her perfect world was going to get even better.

"Up until this point," Marilyn explained, "I hadn't been challenged at all. Ken and I had been living the life we had planned and thought God had intended, but God often provides detours. For us that detour was the birth of our daughter. Joani was born with spina bifida."

For the fifteen days that Joani lived, Marilyn prayed for a miracle cure. The miracle did not come. Rather than welcoming a new daughter into their home, the family planned a funeral. As Marilyn said good-bye to a child she had barely known, she tried to come to grips with why this had to happen. It was at this point that the grieving mother would be revisited by the kind of thinking that had unsettled her as a child.

"As I searched for answers, I visited with a local pastor. He told me to look closely at my own life and my husband's life. He informed me that our sins were the cause of our daughter's death."

The pastor's answer challenged everything she believed in. What sin had she committed, and would God really punish her in that way? The normally positive and upbeat Marilyn sunk deeper into depression as she tried to deal with the tragedy. She felt she had been a good person, a caring Christian, had lived a good life, and she knew her husband was a wonderful man. She always prayed, she was thankful, and she had tried to share her blessings. Yet even though she had done all this, a Christian leader had essentially told her what she had heard time and time again from the grumpy folks in church, "Must have been the sin in her life." Thanks to the positive view of faith taught by her parents, Marilyn, instead of facing adversity like Leroy Walker, who had retreated into his shell, looked for other views that might help her understand the horrific loss she had just experienced.

"It was not my way to do the shell routine. My turtle did that to avoid me, but I did not do that to avoid life. It was not me to go inside and stay there. Still, it really wasn't until Charles Swindoll came to pastor our church and he asked me the question, 'What part do you see God playing in Joani's life?' that I began to understand. God is sovereign, nothing gets past him. He continues to control all things. Things that happen God uses in the design of his grand scheme.

"Up until that point it never occurred to me that God allows the sin to run its course. The original choice that was made (in the garden of Eden) affects everything. Spina bifida is a part of what can come into a life that is no longer perfect."

Marilyn came to realize that in experiences like the death of her daughter, people come to fully understand the ramifications of man's original fall from grace. Getting a handle on the consequences of what happened to Adam and Eve also gave her a new perspective of the death of Jesus. In a step of awareness that went far beyond her knowledge during her original conversion, Marilyn saw that without Christ, everyone would still be constantly trying to provide sacrifices to God to shore up their place with him. So while the pain of Joani's death was incomprehensible, her faith now allowed Marilyn to believe that it was part of God's plan. She even found evidence of this in Ephesians 1:11 (KJV): "Being predestinated according to the purpose of him who worketh all things after the counsel of his own will."

Thus, she no longer had to take inventory of her life trying to find the sin that caused Joani's death. It was not something she and Ken had done. With this foundation of faith, she now accepted that God was good and something good would therefore come out of this tragedy. A year later, when Ken and Marilyn adopted a nine-day-old girl who had been given up by her unmarried teenage parents, Marilyn sensed God's plan was still in place.

"There again we have the grand design," Marilyn explained. "I can't imagine life without Beth, but without the death of our other child, we would have never known her."

For the next two decades, Marilyn's life was back on an idyllic track. She taught English at Biola University for ten years, picked up a master's degree in psychology, and then developed a thriving private practice as a marriage and family counselor. All along the way she assured her children, her friends, her church family, and her patients that God was crazy about them. Yet when she was nearing her fifth decade, the eternally happy, zany woman was faced with the greatest challenge of her life.

"When my husband was diagnosed with pancreatic cancer, we marshaled all our faith troops together. We prayed for a miracle, believing all the while there would be one."

Sadly, the loving, god-natured, gentle man, who laughed his way through his illness as he had his life, died fourteen months after his diagnosis. His passing left Marilyn to wonder why the prayers had not produced the miracle Ken needed.

Sitting alone, Marilyn turned to her Bible. Initially reading God's Word brought more questions than understanding. She even began to wonder why she had ever put much stock in the strange mix of stories woven in between Genesis and Revelation. What if they weren't true? Yet she reasoned there had to be someone who started creation. It couldn't have jump-started itself.

She then concentrated her study on the life of Christ. What if all that she had believed about Jesus was just fiction? Those thoughts tore through her like a knife. She had never felt so alone.

In a move that reflected her many years as a student, she began to dissect the life story of the one she called Lord. As she examined Christ's days on earth, she found historical records outside the Bible that affirmed that Jesus lived. So Christ had been born, he had taught, he had secured a following, and he had been executed. Yet what about the resurrection? Where was the proof of that?

It was at this moment that faith began to seep once more into Marilyn's heart. The tomb of Jesus was empty. A mighty force had rolled away the boulder sealing the grave. He had risen from the dead. If this were not the case, those who crucified him would have produced his body, and those who guarded the tomb would have heard the throng it would have taken to move the stone. So if he had not risen, the rumor could have been quashed before it took root. On top of this fact, none of those who saw the risen Christ turned their backs on him or denied him, even though almost all of them were killed for their belief in Jesus as Lord. If he had not risen, at least one, if not all, would have saved their lives by admitting they had lied. Thus, Marilyn knew by both logic and faith that the story was true. As she came to grips with what she believed, she began to understand more about the deeply personal and painful events that had so impacted her life.

"I didn't know then what I know now," she explained. "If I knew then what I know now—that life slowly unfolds, event by event, and with each event, you learn some new big truth—it would have been easier. I now know that there is no such thing as premature death, that God has assigned each of us a number of days. This thinking is not fatalism, but acknowledging the fact that God is in control. I know Ken died of cancer and he was way too young. He was just fifty-one years old. But I had to come to grips with another aspect of death, that this too was sovereignly ordained."

Losing her life partner was the most radical life-changing event in Marilyn's life. It was compounded by the fact that for the first time in her life, she was truly alone.

"My kids were married. They had both married shortly after Ken died. So I was not just a single mom; I was a single person. I had nobody in the house. That was devastating in the sense that it felt as if I was robbed of all human support. Yet by my nature I knew my life was not done. Not long after Ken died, I was asked to join the Women of Faith speaking team. I wondered if that was a practical move for me. I had to make a living, and I would have to give up my private practice in Newport Beach that was doing very well. I was very secure."

Women of Faith was a brand-new concept. Steve Arterburn, a West Coast pastor, had decided women needed mentors and leaders who reflected a positive faith. He wanted those who spoke for Women of Faith to bring humor and warmth to Christian living. Steve had several people in mind to kick off his venture, and Marilyn was not one of them. It was author Barbara Johnson who recommended that Arterburn include the psychologist in his initial quartet of faithful women. When he heard her speak, he knew Marilyn was essential to making his dream a reality.

For Marilyn, leaving her private practice would take a huge step of faith. With her husband's death and her children gone, it was her practice that brought her some sense of rhythm and security. Yet the more she thought about being able to speak to thousands of women and provide them with the kind of help she was now providing through her practice to just one person at a time, she sensed God's hand pushing her forward.

"I will admit I was worried about failing," she explained. "This was new and fresh. No one knew if it would work. If I made this move, I would have no support from a spouse or parents. I would be out there on my own."

As she contemplated the move and considered what she could bring to the conferences, she realized that everything, from Leroy Walker to the "must have been sin" crowd, to handling the loss of a daughter and husband, had given her the experience to share what living in faith really means. It was almost as if everything that had happened in her life had prepared her for this opportunity. So, knowing she would have to "walk on water," she took down her shingle, closed her practice, and hit the road. Yet even as she encouraged others, making them laugh through their trials, she found herself facing another huge spiritual boulder.

"Ken and I had encouraged Beth from the beginning that if she ever had an interest in tracing her biological roots, we would help her. When she began the search, we did not interpret that as a lack of gratitude or disloyalty of any kind. She had begun the process shortly before Ken was diagnosed with cancer. She dropped it as we talked Ken through his final fourteen months. After he died, she resumed her search."

For Marilyn, watching her excited daughter exuberantly seek out her biological mother and father created natural apprehension. What if these people did not live up to Beth's expectations? What if they didn't want to see her? What if Beth developed a closer relationship with them than she had with Marilyn? Still, just as Marilyn had stepped out in faith when joining Women of Faith, she took another step, believing that God was behind this action too.

"I feel very strongly," Marilyn explained as she looked back on her daughter's search, "that a parent has no right to cling, hang on, or drag down. I will always be the parent. I am in charge in what I communicate in terms of need. My job is to facilitate their needs."

Ultimately it was faith that allowed Marilyn to see both her children in a new light. They weren't really her kids; they were God's children. He had chosen for Marilyn to raise them, but their lives, their future, and their essence were his. That sovereignty doctrine became the down blanket of security Marilyn wrapped around herself during Beth's search. It was also the reason she encouraged her daughter to fight through each roadblock and climb over every hurdle that kept her from reaching her goal. The quest ended in Illinois. The unmarried teenagers who had given Beth up had beaten the odds and stayed together. They had gotten married, gone through college, and surrendered to Christian service. Her birth father was now a Baptist preacher and her birth mother was a dynamic Christian leader. They had a family that reflected their faith. The story could not have had a happier ending for Marilyn, Beth, or the couple.

For over fifteen years Marilyn has been on her own, but never completely alone. God has been there for every step she has taken. The events that brought her hope and heartache have fueled a dozen books (most of which have landed on best seller lists), a series of successful and acclaimed videotape and audiotape projects, and more than three hundred appearances at Women of Faith conferences. She has touched millions with her story, making people cry and think, while also passing on the gift given to her by her father: the ability to laugh through life's battles.

With sound advice, like "You can live a day without chocolate, but you cannot live a day without hope," she has labored through serious illness and great loss. Rarely does she ever seem to concern herself with big or little problems.

"If it weren't for God's sovereignty and my sense of humor, I could get quite anxious about my life," she often explains to those who wonder how she can always smile and never seems to get down. Then she adds, "It's about the fact that when you have your back against the wall, God hears your cry and delivers you from all distress."

Marilyn Meberg has come a long way from her days of trying to leash-train Leroy Walker. Each year she addresses hundreds of thousands with her message of faith. The lesson taught to her by a turtle has helped to sustain her and made it possible for her to inspire millions. That lesson: retreating into your shell in adversity cuts you off from God and the world, and that cuts you off from the faith that can sustain your family, your dreams, your life, and your future. As Marilyn says, "Faith. You can't live without it."

18

MAHALIA JACKSON

Faith to Stay the Course

Unloved as a child, Mahalia found her voice in faith. The fact that she never gave in to the temptations of secular fame actually opened the door for her to experience the worldwide adoration and respect few women have ever known. Her story is about freedom of mind, body, and soul.

By 1971, Mahalia Jackson had been the world's best-known gospel singer for two decades. She had circled the globe several times as a Christian ambassador of hope and compassion. Her voice had charmed presidents, prime ministers, and royalty as well as millions who didn't have a dime. Fans clamored after her by the thousands, begging for autographs and pictures. Television shows around the world featured her performances and wit. Even though she had come from poverty and prejudice to fame and acclaim, Mahalia refused to change. She remained steadfast in her faith and devoted to her Lord. As she had said many times, "I hope to bring people to God with my songs." Certainly the sixty-year-old entertainment icon had accomplished her goal, as millions made their first steps toward Christ when they heard Jackson's dynamic voice. Yet on this September night, as she readied herself for another concert, the energy and vigor that had been a part of every one of her thousands of performances was missing. Mahalia was so tired it seemed she would be unable to pull her large body up off the chair and onto the stage.

The gospel legend had been battling health problems for years. Her heart was failing and, on this night, she was suffering from intestinal and back pain while battling a fever. The woman, who so loved to cook, had lost her appetite. Her friends and advisers wanted Mahalia to cancel this final show and go home to Chicago. They argued that getting rest and medical treatment was far more important than performing. "The fans will understand," they explained. Yet Jackson would not hear of it. She had long lived by a personal creed: "Faith and prayer are the vitamins of the soul; man cannot live in health without them." She believed that if she had enough faith, the strength would come. So she was determined to go on, treating this Munich, Germany, performance as if it were her last chance to share her faith with the world.

It was a frail and trembling Mahalia who rose from her chair and slowly walked on the stage that fall evening. As thousands of adoring fans cried out, she smiled, trying to steady her feet, but nothing seemed to want to work. She was weary, feeling used up and washed out. It was as if old age had suddenly appeared and stolen all the youth from her body and soul. The musicians knew her condition. They were shocked when she did not cancel the performance. Now most of them expected her to sing for a few moments, then beg off. As she stood in a place where a generation before Hitler had preached his demonic messages of hate, they looked for a cue: Was she ready?

Studying the almost worshipful audience, the singer again realized God had given her an awesome responsibility. He had placed in her a talent that built bridges between races and cultures. He had allowed her to be a healing force in her own country and around the world. She knew that through her voice and her life story, she had had the privilege of bringing the story of God to life, proving that good does triumph over evil. It was time to embrace her gift again. With God's help, she could do it.

As she closed her eyes and started to sing "He's Got the Whole World in His Hands," she felt her Lord lifting her up. If was as if she were weightless. Suddenly the strength flowed into her body and her unmatchable voice soared skyward, filling the air with glory that came from deep in the woman's huge heart. Even her feet began dancing the spiritual steps that had always been a part of her performance. The illness that was slowly killing her had been shoved aside, the pain was gone, and Mahalia was praising God. Nothing could stop her now.

Suddenly happy, smiling, and energetic, the Queen of Gospel swept forward, growing stronger with each note. Over the course of the next hour, Jackson belted out song after song, wrapping her voice around each word, embracing each note, and presenting herself to the audience as a woman of God. Through her music she wanted the audience to realize it was faith that had placed her in the spotlight tonight and faith that pushed her on even when her body was too tired to move. She wanted them to leave knowing that faith could do the same for them.

The Munich crowd was awed, coming to their feet time and time again to honor the woman and her message. When she launched into "Just a Closer Walk with Thee," the expression on her face showed the depth of her conviction; her closed eyes presented the singer's sense of God's presence, and the song's message opened the door for others to follow her to Christ. With a mighty clap of her hands and a shout to the heavens, she was living her own motto, "God can make you anything you want to be, but you have to put everything in his hands." Putting herself in his hands was the reason Mahalia could perform on this night and was the only way she could have known any kind of success at all.

As she finished her performance and took a final bow, she stared out at her fans a final time. As they were thanking God for her show, she was thanking him for giving her the strength to complete the performance. She had done it for them. They had wanted to hear her sing gospel music; it was her way of sharing the Lord and preaching. She had unapologetically given them what they wanted. Waving, she turned to leave the stage. Suddenly the world seemed out of focus, as if it was evaporating into a fine, defused mist. She staggered for a moment, trying to find balance on her weak legs, then collapsed. As people gasped, gospel's queen lay on the floor. Weak, disoriented, and unable to stand, Mahalia clung to her faith as she fought to breathe.

Mahalia was from one of the poorest areas of the South. Even before she took her first breath, she had three strikes against her. First, she had been born black in a world controlled by whites. Second, her parents did not have a marriage license; therefore she was relegated to being a member of the lowest class in her own race. And finally, her father, John Jackson, took no interest in his daughter.

Mahalia's mother, Charity, was a maid who worked long hours for wealthy families. Thus the baby spent most of her time with relatives. Crime, prostitution, and despair were her neighbors, and hope was a visitor who rarely showed his face in the neighborhood known as "Black Pearl." The one constant in the family's life was church. It was the Mount Moriah Baptist congregation that would provide the young girl with some stability as well as an early outlet for her talent. Yet even the church family could not ease the stifling grip of poverty or shield the child from a sense of being unwanted.

When Mahalia was five, Charity suddenly grew sick and died. The orphan girl was given to her aunt Mahalia "Duke" Paul. No man, woman, or child dared cross this imposing figure. When she laid down a law, it was followed to the letter. The first rule of the house was that everyone worked and worked hard. The second rule was that nothing but gospel music was to be sung in her home. Mahalia's brother, six aunts, and several half-brothers and half-sisters who lived in the three-room home knew that following Duke's law was the only way to find peace.

When Mahalia came home from school each day, Aunt Duke put her to work. The child was expected to help clean, cook, and wash. After she finished her tasks, they were inspected, often with a white glove. If deemed unsatisfactory, Duke pulled out the belt and used it on the child. Mahalia was then forced to redo what she had failed to do properly the first time. Mahalia Jackson grew up in this harsh world, filled with more discipline than love. Little wonder she often felt like the unwanted stepchild.

Before Mahalia completed eighth grade, Duke forced her to quit school and take a job as a maid. Without an education, it appeared the last chance for the girl to succeed had evaporated. She seemed doomed to relive her mother's short and sad life story.

The church back then offered the only gathering point for poor families. For many, a worship service was little more than a social outlet. But for Mahalia, church and the Bible offered a rich world of joy and hope. In her study, prayer, and singing, she escaped the cruelty of her life. While others talked about God's hand being on their lives, the young girl actually believed it. She sensed that if she had faith, she would be delivered out of a hopeless existence. Every night she prayed that she could find a place where she was wanted and accepted. Little did she know that her family's poverty would be the first answer to her prayers.

By 1927, Duke found she could no longer feed those living in her house, so she deemed her sixteen-year-old niece old enough to be on her own. With little fanfare, the uneducated and insecure Mahalia was pried from the only home she had known and put on a train bound for Chicago. After a three-day ride to the large and frightening city, Mahalia found a relative willing to take her in. The teen then applied for a job washing clothes. Buoyed by prayers that she could make something of herself in spite of her background, she worked long hours and saved enough money to attend the Scott Institute of Beauty Culture.

By the time she was twenty, the Depression had all but killed the economy on Chicago's South Side. Mahalia was working in a beauty shop, at a cleaner's, and as a maid. She lived in a cheap rooming house. She had enough to eat and was not sleeping on the street like many of her friends, so she was thankful for the blessings she had received. Looking for an outlet, she joined the choir at Greater Salem Baptist Church. Never did she dream this simple act would be the initial step to her becoming the best-known African-American woman in the world. In her mind she was just trying to use one of the few gifts God had given her. Other than a ready and willing smile and an untrained but eager voice, Jackson didn't see she had much else to offer.

Salem's choir director immediately noticed Mahalia's rich, strong voice and dynamic range. Initially he gave her some special parts in choral productions. In a matter of months, he moved her to featured soloist. Soon her soaring performances drew more people to the bustling church than did the preacher's sermons. Sensing Mahalia had special spiritual gifts, the pastor teamed her with his three talented sons. For the next seven years this quartet performed at churches throughout the region and created a series of theatrical vignettes. The Singing Johnsons became so well known that when the men decided to give up performing, Mahalia continued to tour, singing at church conventions throughout the Midwest. Since the "love offerings" she was paid for singing did not even cover her rent, she continued to work regular jobs. At the time she never thought about praying for a career as a musical missionary. Considering where she had started, it is little wonder that Jackson didn't feel the need to petition God for any more than she already had.

Faith meant not selling out. Faith meant honoring God by following his lead. Faith meant rejecting what the world wanted even when everyone felt she was throwing away the chance of a lifetime.

In 1936, Jackson married a well-respected college graduate, Isaac "Ike" Hockenhull. Ike had his hand in several different businesses, but sensed that entertainment was where real gold could more easily be mined. Having few personal talents to market, Ike looked to his bride. He had witnessed her performances leave congregations in a trancelike state of joy, but the fact she got next to nothing from it bothered him. He kept driving home the fact that Mahalia needed to stop giving away what she could easily sell. After months of badgering, he finally convinced the woman to audition for a local theater group. When she won a part in *Hot Mikado* by Gilbert and Sullivan, he was thrilled. But the woman with the big voice was not impressed and wouldn't take the part. Performing on stage and singing the blues did not feel right to her. Her refusal to accept the offer put a strain on her marriage. Even as her church friends urged her to opt for a shot at fame, Jackson continued to limit her performances to church. Ike did not take it well. Though it would take many years, his insistence on

Mahalia singing secular music and taking her act to nightclubs would eventually destroy the union.

A year after turning down the part in the musical, temptation again knocked at her door. This time it was the great trumpeter, Louis Armstrong, who sought out the church singer. Louis wanted her to be the headline vocalist on his band's upcoming European tour. He promised Mahalia top dollar if she would join him. The woman replied that God did not give her the voice to throw away on music that had no message.

Decca, the company she had snubbed a year before, came back to Mahalia, this time with an offer that would allow her to sing gospel music. Though her husband felt there would be no money in it, an excited Jackson rushed to the studio to cut "God's Gonna Separate the Wheat from the Tares." The record didn't sell well, earning Jackson just $25 in royalties.

A year later, the "Father of Gospel Music," Thomas A. Dorsey, asked Mahalia to work with him. Dorsey, whose Christian compositions had found wide acclaim and broken many color lines, was the most respected gospel musician in the nation. With Dorsey, Jackson gained a new audience, performing at denominational conventions and in the nation's largest African-American churches. This teaming would result in Mahalia being named the official voice of the National Baptist Convention and land her a recording contract with Apollo Records. In 1946, the singer's stubborn faith was proven rock solid as she sold more than two million copies of the single "Move On Up a Little Higher." The record did more than put Jackson on the national map; for the first time it placed gospel music in the national eye.

By 1950, Mahalia had earned major success in her genre, but she was still a performer that few understood or knew how to handle. If she had been white, doors would have opened, but as a black woman, she still found herself waiting at the back of the line.

Even as a successful artist, Jackson discovered that in the four decades since her birth, little had changed. America was still segregated and blacks were still viewed as second-class citizens. While her music was enjoyed by white audiences, she was refused service at many hotels and restaurants. The simple fact that she was a woman of color seemed to limit her potential. On top of being black, she sang gospel music. There were few outlets for those who embraced strictly songs of faith. With those odds against her, many in the media predicted that Jackson would be a one-hit wonder, a flash in the pan who would quickly go back to her beauty shop in Chicago. Those who dismissed her because of her color and the seemingly limited potential of her music underestimated the power of her voice and her unique style.

In spite of everything against her, she succeeded. Because of her dynamic vocals, Jackson was booked at Carnegie Hall in 1950—the first time the hallowed venue had featured gospel music. Those who came to the concert had never been exposed to anything like Mahalia Jackson. Even before they realized what she was singing, they were drawn in by her originality. She attacked a song, played with the phrasing, allowed her spirit to guide her rhythm, and never rushed the underlying message. After her appearance at Carnegie Hall, Mahalia was featured on Ed Sullivan's nationally televised *Toast of the Town*. Harry Truman had her perform at the White House. And due to great critical reviews gained on a national tour of large churches and concert halls, Jackson was booked on a tour of Europe. She followed her sold-out foreign performances with several hit gospel recordings.

For reasons that no one in the media seemed to understand, Jackson became a huge star. Millions who would not watch other black entertainers on television or view any religious programming, eagerly tuned in when Mahalia was a guest on network variety shows. Performers such as Nat King Cole and Dinah Shore, who normally did not sing Christian music, lined up to sing duets with Mahalia on gospel classics. Symphonies and orchestras asked her to front for them, and Louis Armstrong, Percy Faith, and even Harpo Marx found ways to join the gospel legend on stage. She appeared in several Hollywood films where, as per her contract, she always sang a song of faith. In 1958, she even headlined at the famed Newport Jazz Festival, singing gospel music, accompanied by Duke Ellington and his band.

One by one, she was overcoming the odds, breaking down the doors, and pushing her Christian message into the mainstream without ever compromising her values. And she accomplished it all with no apologies. When John F. Kennedy asked her to sing at his presidential inauguration, it seemed that Jackson had escaped all that pain and suffering of her youth. She had proven her husband, her friends, and the critics wrong; she had been recognized on her merits and on her outspoken faith. The color of her skin had not held her back.

Even as she achieved worldwide acclaim, many African Americans believed that Mahalia's success was due to the fact her happy face, round figure, and sweet religious songs had been deemed safe by the white establishment. Many who were laboring for civil rights and an end to segregation strongly felt that Jackson represented the "good and obedient Negro." Some at her record company and many of her advisers pushed her to fully embrace this image and asked her not to get involved in the civil rights demonstrations that were starting to pop up around the nation. But Mahalia, believing that God wanted her to use her success to lift up others, jumped at the chance to lend her voice to the movement. If this meant she would be blacklisted and her career would dry up, she argued that she could always go back to singing in a church choir and working in a beauty shop.

Mahalia first stood up for the cause of civil rights during the Montgomery, Alabama, bus boycott in 1955. She sang at several rallies, often leading the crowd in the old gospel standard "We Shall Overcome." As television news coverage was in its infancy, few outside of the Montgomery area realized the gospel singer had participated in the events. So it would be eight years later before Jackson's stand would gain notice.

In the early sixties, Martin Luther King Jr. became the greatest voice in the civil rights movement. On August 28, 1963, at the mall in Washington, D.C., 200,000 gathered to protest the racial divide in the United States. The speakers at the rally argued it was time for equality to be finally and fully recognized. Just before the main address, Mahalia stood up and sang the old spiritual "I Been 'Buked and I

Been Scorned." Her rich voice and sincere delivery were heard by tens of millions who watched on network television. Jackson's dramatic performance was a perfect prelude to the most important moment in African-American history. Martin Luther King Jr. was partway through his speech when Jackson yelled out, "Tell them about the dream!" Picking up on the cue, King launched into a message he had given many times before. This time he mesmerized the world with his "I Have a Dream" speech.

Many now look back on the Washington March as the victory bell for the civil rights movement. Mahalia Jackson had prayed for that day in August to be the final blow needed to finish off the prejudice that stalked blacks all their lives. Yet in truth, King's speech was just the beginning. The call for equal rights was met with violence. The gospel singer saw it as a fight for the soul of America. In the years that followed that monumental rally, evil was often stronger than good.

First John F. Kennedy was shot. Losing the president devastated Jackson, who sang on national television the night of his death to honor the fallen leader. Martin Luther King Jr. was assassinated next. Though Mahalia found the strength to sing "Take My Hand, Precious Lord" at his funeral, the death of her friend shook her to the core. Soon after, Bobby Kennedy was gunned down.

The spiritual depression that Mahalia experienced as a result of the civil unrest was compounded by health problems. Jackson, whose weight hovered between 250 and 300 pounds, was suffering from a variety of issues, the most serious being a heart ailment. Yet she would not cut back on her schedule. India's leader Indira Gandhi wanted her to perform in India. The government even promised Mahalia her performances would be open to people of all the different castes. No gospel singer had ever been asked to perform large-scale concerts in that region, and Mahalia was not going to miss the opportunity to share her Christian faith with these people.

Japan extended an invitation to headline a concert tour in that nation. Jackson also was asked to spend time with the country's royal family. Again, her talent had opened doors for her faith, and she was not going to let such an opportunity slide by.

And the requests kept coming. England wanted her to perform at Prince Albert Hall and give a command performance for the queen. In Paris, where she was called "The Angel of Peace," thousands had already registered for tickets for her next tour. In Germany they begged her to make appearances in all the nation's major cities. Several countries in Africa wanted her to sing as well. "If God was dead," Jackson proclaimed, then why did so many want to hear her sing his music?

The requests she fulfilled led her to the final concert in Munich. Jackson survived her collapse on the German stage and made it back home to Chicago. She died on January 27, 1972, knowing she had never sold out, never gave up, and never shortchanged her calling. She was always foremost a Christian and, no matter where she traveled, she never apologized for singing about Jesus. Her voice was loud, but her actions were louder. She may have once been the unwanted child, the little girl who had been passed around, the woman who embraced faith when no one would embrace her, the stubborn rebel who would not give up her message for fame, but she lived to be embraced by the world. In the process she broke down doors for women, for her race, and for the faith she exported around the globe. Mahalia Jackson proved that with God there are no limits or barriers.

19

MARY DUNHAM FAULKNER

Faith to Follow an Unmarked Road

For most of her life her path to becoming a part of God's work was an easy one, yet it was when everything crumbled that Mary found the voice and courage to take her faith to women all around the world. This is the story of losing it all and finding a real calling.

She never actually had a home, at least not the conventional type that always stayed in one place. She and her ten brothers and sisters were raised on the road. In her first ten years of life Mary Dunham had traveled to every state in the union and several foreign countries. Home was a travel trailer, a hotel room, the back room at a church. The family kitchen was often a campfire, and school took place at whatever table happened to be in the vicinity. There was no television, no permanent address, and no telephone. The family was essentially a gypsy clan, following the wind, always looking for the next place to light.

John Dunham, "Daddy" as his family called him, loved the bottle as much as he loved life. Drinking was his passion and getting drunk his daily goal. That all changed when the out-of-work laborer attended a revival. The preacher's words, combined with his wife's fervent prayers, got through to Daddy that night. His cloudy mind cleared as he woke up to his own sorry state. He realized that as a drunk he was giving his wife and small daughter nothing but grief. They were starving for security, hope, and stability. As he inventoried his accomplishments, he found little of which he could be proud. Yes, he admitted, he had to change, but he simply didn't know a way to do it. He craved alcohol. He had to have it. Booze controlled his mind and soul. Without a drink he fell into a panic, lost all his focus, and the world became hopeless. When he drank he felt like he was somebody. When he was sober he knew the truth. So he couldn't give up booze; it was the crutch that supported his whole world. But, what a miserable world it was.

"God help me," he whispered as the invitation played. Somewhere he heard a voice assuring him that "I will help you." Still, getting up and walking forward took the kind of courage he only found in a bottle. "Where's a drink when you need it?" he wondered. Unsure what to do or say, Dunham rose to his feet. In faltering steps he moved toward the preacher. Falling to his knees he admitted his sins, asked for forgiveness, and promised to change. He told himself his confession was sincere, but he still wondered what would happen the next time he craved a drink.

When the urge to drink revisited him, the newly saved man prayed. To further push the urge to the back of his mind, he read the Bible. He sensed his feeble attempts at escaping the grip of addiction were not enough. To fully turn his back on his old life, he needed a new one. The best way to resist temptation, he thought, would be by giving himself to Christian service. Once again falling to his knees, he asked God for direction. Again he heard a voice. This time the marching orders were clear: "There is a forty-foot highway out there; start traveling and you will find all you need."

Even in his drunken stupors, Dunham had never considered anything this outlandish. He didn't own a car and had no money. There was no way he could start serving God by just aimlessly hitting the road. But the voice would not allow him to rest. It kept prodding him to take his family and start walking down that rural Montana highway. Finally, after packing the few belongings they had, Daddy and CeCelia, along with their infant daughter, picked up two ragged suitcases and headed west. Eventually a trucker gave them a ride. The first night they stopped at a church and worshiped. The pastor gave them enough money for food and let them stay in the church building. They hit the road again and made it to Billings. A trucker dropped them off in front of a storefront church. That night John preached his first sermon. As God's promise had proven, he was providing for them. The Dunhams kept praying, moving, and looking for the next place someone needed to hear God's Word. They did not quit until John died.

More than a decade after her father's conversion, Mary was born into the ministry. Even as an infant she was in church every night and on the road almost every day. As millions of Americans were buying televisions and tuning in to view the black-and-white images, the little girl was seeing the country close-up, one tiny town at a time. Every day the landscape changed, each new service was unique, and every new experience became a treasure stored in a memory. As she grew, learning to play the piano and sing with her siblings, Mary became an active part of the ministry. Churchyards were her playgrounds and worship services her entertainment. She made new friends at every stop and lost them a day, a week, or a month later. Yet she didn't mind nor did she feel cheated. For the bright sandy-haired little girl, life was perfect.

Mary idolized her father. She could see that he was not only living his call but constantly studying to learn even more about that call. She learned about sacrifice, respect, and honor from his actions. She sensed the joy of ministry from the way he looked forward to each new service and welcomed each new convert to the knowledge of Christ.

From her mother, Mary learned the power of prayer. CeCelia was so firmly anchored in her relationship with God that she seemingly never doubted anything. If there was no money, she still believed that the Lord would provide food. Once, in Tibet, when angry hordes were threatening to kill them, CeCelia remained calm. She told those around them that if God was with her, then she was safe. Mary sensed the strong faith her mother possessed was because of the deep communication she had with her Lord. Thus, from her mother she learned the real power of prayer.

Mary watched her older brothers and sisters grow up on the road, then depart to obtain a more formal education. As close as she was to her family, leaving the ministry was something she dreaded. She relished the nights of praise, she loved the music, and she felt secure in the midst of the constant movement. Then, just after she entered her teens, it was time to take her first independent step.

"My father was associated with a small interdenominational bible college in San Antonio. They had a high school section that was a boarding school. When I was fourteen I went to school there."

The International Bible School offered Mary her first grounded home. The lack of movement took some getting used to. She missed the travel, meeting new people, and being actively involved in nightly services. Yet the school did offer her a chance to make long-term friends and get a grip on all the elements of American life she had missed. Suddenly she became aware of modern music, clothes, and television programs. She also began to see boys in a new light.

"I met Dan when I was fourteen," Mary recalled. "He was in bible college. Over time we started dating. When I finished high school and he finished college, he asked me to marry him."

Though she was still a few months short of her seventeenth birthday, Mary was sure she loved Dan Faulkner. Her parents approved as well. Still, no one expected the two to immediately jump into marriage. Yet circumstances beyond their control would set in motion a very quick union.

"Dan was associated with the Life Tabernacle in Louisiana," Mary explained. "The church was very well known at that time. Two members of the congregation, Don and Anna Jean Price, were going to Thailand for missionary service. They asked Dan to go with them. I was suddenly given a choice. I could get married immediately or wait until he came back in five years. I chose to get married then and go with him to Thailand."

In 1964, as the newlyweds packed their bags, the world was going through dramatic change. The Faulkners were traveling to an area ripe with conflict. The war in Vietnam was escalating; Communist China was perched to push its ideology into other Southeast Asian nations; World War III seemed to be just a blink of an eye away. Innocent, ignorant, and unprepared, the Faulkners made a huge step of faith. In a very real sense, Mary was repeating what her father had done some three decades before. Undaunted by the challenge of what was in front of them, the young couple boarded a plane and traveled halfway around the globe to start a mission in the heart of this unstable area.

"My husband and I were in Thailand for twenty-five years. We established a girls' home, several village churches, and raised three children there. Our work was blessed and we loved it."

The couple came back home in 1989 to put their son in college. Mary anticipated being in the States a year or so, then going back to the nation that had literally become her home.

"When we returned we had three children who hardly knew their aunts and uncles, but were very connected to the Thai culture. Everything was brand-new to them. We bought a house, worked at getting the children established, and stayed in touch with our work in Thailand. The work we had started was booming and I was looking forward to getting back.

"Yet, I knew something was wrong. I couldn't put a handle on it, but I knew we had problems. Dan wouldn't talk about it. Then one day, just out of the blue, he told me that he was in love with a Thai woman. I knew her. She was one of my friends."

Mary was destroyed. The only man she had ever dated, a man she had complete trust in, was now rejecting her. He wanted to give up everything in order to be with this other woman. She didn't know what to do. Nothing in her life had prepared her for this moment.

"Even admitting our problems to friends, to pastors was hard," Mary admitted. "When we did, they would tell us, 'Don't talk about it. There's a place in Cleveland that you can go to for help.' My children were dazed, in culture shock, and then they discovered Dad has a mistress. They knew her and had called her 'aunt.'"

Mary had lived her whole life in the ministry. She had never faced a serious personal problem. She had never been given an issue that she couldn't take care of through prayer and hard work. Thus, she set about trying to fix her marriage in the same way she had addressed all the other traumas she had faced on the mission field.

"'I can keep him,' I convinced myself, 'if I really pray, lose weight, and get more godly. I can save this.' So I spent a year thinking this was just a bad patch and I could fix it. All the while I kept the lie in. In fact Dan and I continued to send out glowing reports to our supporters about our ministry. It was true the ministry was going well, but things were falling apart at home."

In Mary's mind, divorce was a horrible sin. So even when her husband did not want to try to make their marriage work, she would not give up on it. She was determined to fix it. Then her father died and zapped her fragile optimism. The one man she knew she could always trust and lean on was gone. When she returned to Dallas from the funeral, she discovered the mortgage company was foreclosing on their home. She asked Dan what they would do. He answered by getting on a plane for Thailand. Mary was now convinced her usefulness as a Christian worker was over.

"I had been in ministry since I was a child. I knew how to act and what to do in ministry. But put me in Dallas, Texas, and tell me to start over and I didn't know how to do it. I had never had a job or a career; I had only done ministry."

Her children were the only things that kept Mary from sinking into a hopeless depression. Her older daughter was married and her son was in college, but she still had one daughter in junior high school. As a mother she had to find a way to provide food, clothing, and shelter. With no marketable skills, it wasn't going to be easy. To Mary this step of faith seemed larger than even moving to Thailand as a teenage bride.

Mary landed a job answering phones at American Airlines. The job paid enough for her to rent a small deserted home in the slums. Surrounded by crime and desperation, she and her daughter did not so much live as survive.

"The amazing thing was, I was not angry with God. When you are overseas and don't have anyone feeding you, you learn to feed yourself at an early age. I just knew how to get in the Word, keep myself very focused. My faith never wavered.

"But when this happened, I could not stand to be around the church. It was full of platitudes and that killed me. I grew very tired of people flinging out phrases. If you don't know what you are talking about, don't say it. If it has not been tried in the fire, I didn't want to hear it. So rather than go to church, I stayed home and studied my Bible on Sunday morning."

Most people trying to get back still hang onto dreams. Mary had no real dreams. Serving God was not only all she knew but all she wanted to do. Thus living without dreams was becoming more and more of a struggle. In spite of her lack of excitement about life, she quickly advanced in her job. Within a year of starting at American Airlines, Mary was supervising fifty people.

"During this time," Mary recalled, "American was involved in economic problems and was laying off scores of people. They assured me I would not be one of them. In fact they offered me a great new position. I begged them to let me go. I knew I didn't belong there."

Those around Mary sensed she had finally lost it. She had given up the only anchor she had. And when she tried to explain that she felt this is what God wanted her to do, the few friends she had thought she was crazy.

"I was living in the slums, taking care of my thirteen-year-old daughter, and had no job. I would just go out and walk, praying, 'God I have to have my inheritance, I have to have what's mine.'"

During one of her daily strolls, Mary flashed back to her father's funeral. She had spoken at that service, and after the burial a pastor had pulled her to one side and said, "Mary you have a call of God on your life."

"When I reconsidered what the pastor told me, I thought, 'God sees me. He cares for me. He has a place for me.' At that point I started praying a different prayer. Instead of 'Poor me, I don't have money, a dad, a home, or a ministry,' I switched to 'How can you use me, God?'"

A few days later Mary was again walking when she stopped to watch a woman working in a flower garden outside a beautiful old home. The woman got up off her knees and greeted Mary. They talked for a while before the gardener asked, "What do you do?"

Without thinking, Mary answered, "I'm a minister."

"Really. Then why don't you come and speak at my church this Sunday?"

A shocked Mary argued, "You don't even know me. What if I'm a serial killer? How can you know I will do a good job? And don't you have to get permission?"

"I can arrange it," the woman assured her.

In one day, during one chance meeting, God confirmed that he could open doors even for a divorced Mary if she was willing to hit the road and start walking.

The first speaking engagement went very well and led to another. Others called and asked her to speak to their groups, and Mary believed she could live and survive with no regular salary. It was not like being on the mission field, but at least she was again talking about God and faith.

One of the first women of influence who took an interest in Mary's story was the wife of the first owner of the Dallas Cowboys, Anne Murchison, a dynamic Christian woman who devoted her time and money to spreading the gospel. In Mary she saw a woman who had nothing but faith, but Anne sensed that was more than enough. Anne brought Mary in to help with several of her projects. She became so impressed with the former missionary's passion for God and her gift of expression, she asked Mary to write a book with her.

"I was with Anne," Mary recalled, "when the story of genocide in Rwanda came up in the news. The report spoke of how many under-eighteen-year-old heads of households there were in the nation. Before then I had never heard of Rwanda, but I felt a call to get to know more about the country. Anne introduced me to a friend who was an African minister. He asked me to conduct a women's seminar with Anne in Kenya. I couldn't believe it. After the mess that had happened in

Thailand, I never thought the door back into the nations would open for me.

"I didn't have the money, but I went anyway. My luggage was stolen and my plane was late. I was dirty, tired, and in a daze when I went to my first meeting. As I sat there and looked around, I suddenly remembered a movie my folks had shown me called *Black Gold*. It was about Christian work in Africa. I remembered that as I watched that movie as a child, I had promised myself that someday I would go to Africa for God. And here I was."

Mary had told her life story in churches throughout Texas, but in Africa she needed a new way to reach people, a message they could relate to. As she studied the book of Esther, God didn't just speak to her, he gave her a way to use her own situation to help others gain self-esteem and faith.

"I read the story of Rachel and Leah and saw it in a new light. I immediately identified with Leah because she was the cross-eyed ugly sister while Rachel was the pretty one. Yet Leah did so much. In fact Christ came not through Rachel's lineage but through Leah's. With that in mind, I got the idea to start a ministry that would bring together the sisterhood of broken and bruised women."

After hearing Mary speak of Leah's life and her own struggles, a group of Rwandan ministers approached the former missionary. They asked her to address a women's conference in their country. A new door was opening and, even knowing the dangers of tribal violence, Mary took another step of faith.

"Genocide was still raw," Mary recalled, "and people were still afraid to go into Rwanda. We met in a little school, and many of these women had traveled by foot twenty and thirty miles just to meet with us. One woman told me she had lost sixteen family members in one day. Another young woman explained she had seen her mother and children beheaded. Everyone had a story. My life was immediately changed. It was so amazing! I had found a whole nation of Leah's sisters. I had to do something for these women. I met the pastor of the largest church in Kigali, Rwanda, and told him this is what I am called to do."

With no money, Mary pledged to provide a new life for those decimated by the tribal genocide in Rwanda. She rushed back to the United States and formed the organization "Leah's Sisters." In churches across the nation she spoke of the horrors she had seen and the faith that was alive in these people who had lost everything. Mary became one of the first and loudest voices of awareness on the cause of Rwanda. And when others moved on to new problem areas, she stayed to continue to heal the wounds she found there, raising money for schools and clinics. As more than 70 percent of the population was female, she expanded her work by setting up workshops and education programs. Soon her focus became raising up a new generation of female Christian leaders to bring hope, peace, and security to Rwanda.

Mary's message of hope and determination had been born out of her own life experiences. In one quick swoop, the world had seemingly taken away everything but her faith. She was divorced, embarrassed, and ashamed. Her personal failures seemed to doom her from ever doing God's work again. Yet even during this test, she never doubted that he continued to be there for her. And when she was challenged to take a new leap of faith, he rewarded her large step.

Mary's successful mission to build female Christian leaders in Rwanda was soon noted by several different mission organizations. As they watched women who had been brutalized rebuild their lives and their communities, representatives from across the world asked Mary to come to their countries to help establish her program. Within five years of landing in Africa, she was leading conferences for scarred women in Burma, Kenya, South America, eastern Europe, and Cambodia. Mary Dunham Faulkner continues to this day going into areas filled with unknown danger while living on the road of faith where her father found his calling.

20

AN UNKNOWN WOMAN OF FAITH

This book began with a look at someone whose name and story you did not know. As that was a good place for a beginning, I feel a need to end the book by spotlighting a woman whose name none of us will ever know. In this story of faith, a remarkable man overcomes great odds to achieve greatness. Yet without the impact of a woman whose face he never saw, whose age he never knew, and whose name he never asked, Gene would have forever remained blind to his own talents and potential. She was in a sense the Good Samaritan, but she was also much more. She was what every Christian should be: a cheerleader, an encourager, a person whose faith builds a bridge from hopelessness to real hope. In the midst of great tragedy, she was the unseen light and the unknown angel. What her faith gave birth to is simply amazing.

On May 26, 1967, the sergeant and 104 of his fellow foot soldiers crossed a grassy Vietnam plain just a few miles from the Cambodian border. It had been weeks since any of them had seen any signs of an enemy, and this lack of activity had lulled Gene and the men around him into a false sense of security. The Asian daytime heat, coupled with the nighttime cold, the never-ending monsoon rains, and the waves of angry mosquitoes, had become his most stubborn foes. The enemy was pushed as far back in his head as were the lazy summers of his youth in the Ozark Mountains.

At 9:30 a.m. the men paused for a break. As the war now seemed a thousand miles away, Gene found himself thinking of the hills and fishing streams of his hometown, Alton, Missouri. He had no idea that as he daydreamed, a well-hidden enemy was watching his every move. In the time it takes to blink, his whole world would be turned upside down.

As Gene was taking off his rucksack, he heard something to his right. Before he could turn his head, a burst of rifle fire reawakened him to the fact he was fighting a war. Instinct took over as Gene immediately flung himself behind a rotten log and put his rucksack in front of his face for cover. Shots continued to rain down on him. Gene saw the smoke and heard the noise of battle, but he could not see the enemy. Bullets continued to spray the area where he lay, but he held his fire and searched in the trees and grass for the enemy. It was as if his foe were invisible. The men trying to kill him were completely hidden. As he frantically searched the horizon all around him, his buddies were falling, one by one. A feeling of helplessness and hopelessness enveloped him. Another friend fell, and blood spray landed on Gene. Panic set in. This would be it. Within days of being shipped back home, he was sure he was going to die.

Leaning up over his cover, Gene again tried to find the source of the gunfire. He studied the scene in front of him as carefully as he had ever looked at anything. In seconds he recorded every movement in the brush, the way the trees swayed in the wind, and even the shadows created by the sun playing down on the trees. If death and destruction had not been hidden in this picture, what he saw would have been a wonderful postcard. And that was the irony of what his eyes took in: in the midst of a beautiful world was unforgiving death. Little did he know that this scene would be the last thing he would ever see.

Without warning, another puff of smoke popped up in front of him. A crashing noise was followed by a sharp pain in the side of his head. A split second later he was knocked flat on his back as death tried to slowly push its way through his body.

Though he could not comprehend what had just transpired, those around him realized that Gene had been shot in the forehead by a round that went through his helmet and into his skull. Now blind, his buddies unable to fight through the fire to get to him, Gene found the strength to grope in his rucksack for his first aid pouch.

After finding it, he stuck a piece of cloth in the hole in his forehead and wiped away the blood with his other hand. He was shocked when he realized that he still couldn't see. Believing his sightlessness was due to the unrelenting bleeding, he turned over to keep the blood from running into his eyes. It was then he was shot again. This time a bullet sliced through his foot. Instinctively, he rolled back over. As he did he felt shrapnel from an artillery round pierce his left shoulder. Gene realized he was a target and knew that in the next few minutes one more round could punch his ticket to the next world.

For the next hour, fearing that he was going to be run over and stabbed in the back, Gene kept reloading his rifle and firing blindly in the direction where he thought the enemy was hiding. He had no idea how the battle was going or how badly he was injured. All he knew was fear and all he expected was death. By noon, perhaps satisfied they had inflicted enough damage, the enemy retreated. Medics arrived in helicopters to recover the wounded and the dead. Gene, now exhausted and in shock, was placed on one of the first flights out. However, it wasn't until midnight that he was rolled into an emergency room at a military hospital in South Vietnam. It was only then he would begin to grasp how badly he had been hurt.

A doctor said, "I'm going to shine a flashlight into your eyes. Tell me when it's on and when it's not." A few seconds later the doctor asked, "Do you see it now?"

"Yes," Gene assured him.

"How about now?"

"No."

"Okay, that's all I need to know at this time." The doctor moved on to the next patient, leaving Gene alone to consider what had just happened. He was sure he had seen a light; it might have been faint, but it was there. Later that night, Gene found out that the doctor had never turned the flashlight on. When he had walked away from the badly injured soldier, the physician had told his surgical crew, "Remove the eyes." Yet Gene had passed out before he could be told that verdict. He would not wake up for several days.

When Gene did finally awaken, he was in Japan. It was two days before his twenty-first birthday when he learned his optic nerve had been severed by a bullet that crashed through his helmet. His eyes were gone; there was no hope of ever seeing again.

Initially Gene considered suicide. To him, his life already was over. Besides, he reasoned, it had never been much of a life anyway. Even before he had been dealt this blow, the shy Missouri farm boy had expected little from himself. In large part, this was due to the ridicule he had received from his father, who constantly told him he was "stupid, lazy, untalented, and worthless," ending with "and you will never amount to anything." Gene couldn't figure out why his dad hated him. He always tried his best, but even when he succeeded at something, it was never good enough. Eventually he gave up at home.

The one thing that Gene was good at was basketball. He was the star of his team and the talk of the region. Missouri offered him a scholarship to play for the Tigers, and he gladly escaped the farm and his father to go to Columbia. Yet his father's shadow followed him, and Gene soon convinced himself he was not smart enough for the academic side of college. After a while, he quit trying. When Gene flunked out of college, his self-esteem, fueled only by basketball, disappeared. He now completely mirrored his father's image of him. If he lacked self-confidence before he lost his sight, how could he possibly, now that he was blind, overcome this additional hurdle?

Given a set of dark glasses that drew more attention to his handicap, Gene spent months in various Veterans Administration hospitals in countless rehabilitation training sessions. In most of those facilities he was given little hope as employees merely tried to give him just enough skills to get around a house on his own. Yet in the myriad of people who worked with him, there was one voice that went beyond the call of her job. She was determined to make sure Gene actually saw something special in himself. As he had been blind to his potential even before the bullet crashed into his head, this nurse had a big job in front of her. Even though Gene greeted her less than enthusiastically, she was not deterred.

"Hello, Gene, how are you doing?"

Gene could hear the smile in her greeting, but rarely returned it with much more than a mumble. Over time, as her cheery voice continued to call out to him, he began to imagine her as a pretty, petite cheerleader type. As he warmed up, so did she.

"You are really doing well," she told him as she watched him in therapy.

"Thanks," Gene replied.

Over the next few weeks the nurse began to stop by and talk to Gene. She listened as he told her about his life, his failures, his fears, and his desire to simply die. He said he had been worthless, dumb, and lost even when he could see. Now he was simply a burden on society, a person who would have been better off bleeding to death in Vietnam.

The nurse listened, considered the man's thoughts, and began to show him ways he stood out from those around him. She told him how smart he was, how quickly he was mastering moving around on his own and reading Braille. She also informed him he was good looking, had a great smile, and that she felt God had plans for him.

Gene took in her words, but believed few of them. He especially did not believe that the world, much less God, would have any use for him. Yet the nurse would not give up. She sought and found more and more ways to show Gene his potential. By the time he left her ward, he actually believed he might find a place where he could fit in. She had encouraged him to go back to school. He was smart. She assured him he had proven it to her time and again in their conversations. She also told him he would be able to see things with his heart. "Keep listening to your heart," she begged him, "and keep praying, because I will be praying for you."

He left the VA with optimism, but when he returned to Missouri, the young man was plunged into a new round of hopelessness. Without his cheerleader assuring him he had a place in the world, he grew angry, bitter, and frustrated. Realizing just how limited he was and dealing with the opinions of others on the way handicapped individuals are supposed to function beat him down so far he again thought of suicide. The nurse's words forgotten, he refused to accept his blindness and didn't want to learn job skills necessary to function as a blind person.

It took several years before Gene thought back to his nurse and her belief in him. As he considered her interest in him, her encouragement, he began to wonder if she had been sent by God to push him in the right direction. But what direction was that? She had tried to convince him he was smart. He had already flunked out of one school. Expecting very little, he enrolled in St. Louis University, and he quickly discovered that his nurse had been right. He wasn't dumb. His grades placed him near the top of his class.

Between that fateful day in Vietnam and 1977, he received an undergraduate degree and studied law, worked as a marriage counselor, and sustained the life of a successful, independent professional. Gene was respected and self-sufficient. Yet a war was still being waged within his soul. He wanted the world to notice how far he had come, to have his father congratulate him, and to unleash his full potential. Yet he sensed blindness was going to block any of that from happening. Just as before, Gene buried his problems in his heart and bitterness again ruled his emotions. He was good at seeing other people's problems, good at advising them to open up and deal with the issues controlling their lives, but he still hadn't confronted his own self-image problem. What he needed was the nurse to enter his office and assure him again that he was worthy of success and that God really did love him. Instead, he was surrounded by people bent on placing limits on his life.

Drawing from the nurse's idea of seeing with his heart, Gene began to take inventory of why he felt so unsuccessful and unhappy. He found that for a decade he had blamed his blindness for his disillusioned view of life. He began to understand that his real problem centered on the way he looked at himself. Gene didn't fear being blind.

What he feared was that his father had been right and the nurse had been wrong. She was the only person who had ever had the faith to believe his life had any real potential or value.

His nurse had assured him that he did not die in Vietnam because God had a plan for him. She had tried to convince Gene that God loved him. The problem that now faced him was, could he believe that as strongly as she had? As he thought about her words, he whispered, "I really believe that God is good and loving and created me and has a purpose for me. Yet, how much stock do I really put in him if I don't like myself, one of his creations?"

The nurse had liked Gene, he was sure of that. She had believed in him too. But why? What had given her such faith? Gene then realized it was God. God had been there for Gene through her words, her compassion, and her interest. And wherever she was, she was still praying for him. He just knew that. Maybe, he thought, it was time to pray for himself.

With this new insight, Gene cleared his first big hurdle. Suddenly he realized that his blindness and those it had brought into his life had made him look at himself with a different scrutiny, something he probably would not have done if he could still see. His blindness had shown him that God lives and had given him the ability and the motivation to like himself. This understanding and faith, first spoken by someone he would never see, gave Gene the first positive outlook he had ever known.

To many people, it seemed that Gene had already conquered many challenges, but earning his degree, holding his job, and maintaining his independence had only been attempts to get others to notice that he wasn't all the bad things he had grown up to believe he was. These accomplishments hadn't changed his view of himself. This was what others wanted him to do and be. Now he wanted to do things God's way. But to accomplish this new goal he had to see with his heart.

When Gene realized that God wanted him to set his own goals and live his own dreams, he stopped being a self-centered, struggling blind person. He began to see his own potential and the potential he had to reach others. He realized that the first step in fulfilling his potential was simply to like himself!

In 1979, while still a counselor, he bought a four-unit apartment complex in an effort to expand his horizons and gain another source of income. People told him he couldn't possibly take care of it, but he believed he could. Gene had no difficulty collecting rent, dealing with tenants, or renting vacant units. He did have one headache common to many landlords: he couldn't get competent people to fix the broken appliances and leaky plumbing. So he taught himself how to make these repairs.

Success breeds success and self-confidence. Within three years, Gene bought several apartment complexes, fixed them up (usually doing the work himself), and leased the units. One night a really crazy idea settled in his head. He decided that if he could run and oversee a large number of apartments, then he could build a house. Calling on friends within the construction business for subcontract work, he designed and built his first home. When it sold, he built another house, this one a little bigger and with more luxury features. Then came another and another.

Gene discovered that not being able to see didn't stop him from visualizing how things should be. He could "feel" his plans better than most people could see them. He could check a subcontractor's work with his hands better than anyone could check it with their eyes. Furthermore, he hired men he trusted, men who would not cut corners.

Within five years, Gene's homes became known as some of the best built in the St. Louis area. As one subcontractor explained to a reporter, "Gene sees designs that we have never done because his imagination is not limited by conventional sight. He dreams new dreams. But even more than this, he feels things that are wrong, things we simply overlook. He also constantly studies and listens, always keeping up with the new trends, and then he adds his own touch. His homes are not only well built, they are originals."

But there is more to Gene than just being a builder of fine homes. Anyone who meets him quickly picks up on this. It was a crisp morning in October when I first met Gene Mauldin. He was sitting in his office located in his newest development, an area filled with sloping hills, large colorful trees, and a tranquil lake. All around him was nature at its most beautiful. It was an area that he had discovered and purchased, then divided into three-acre homesites. The homes that will eventually fill this subdivision will represent some of Gene's finest work.

Before I spoke with him, he had had meetings with his subcontractors, joined a building inspector on a final tour of his most recently completed home, answered numerous phone calls, and spent the time in between meetings and calls mapping out the details for the remainder of the homes he was building in this subdivision. Yet, in the middle of this heavy schedule, Gene paused, looked up a phone number on his Braille notepad, and called a young woman he had met a few weeks before. Jane had recently lost her sight because of severe juvenile diabetes. A mutual friend had introduced them, and since that first meeting, Gene had checked on her from time to time just to give her a spiritual boost. Sharing people's burdens and helping them rediscover their potential is something he feels called to do. And why not? This type of input by a woman in his past was the first step he took in not just recovering but in understanding how much he and God could accomplish together.

Those around Gene laughingly say that he spends as much time rebuilding people as he does building homes. At one time Gene had lost the will to live and the motivation to dream. So, better than most, he can identify with someone who has given up. Just as someone touched him, he reaches out because he wants each forgotten person to know what it takes to pull oneself back up and the exhilaration one feels when success is achieved.

As he talks with the young blind woman, he can sense her hopelessness waning and her enthusiasm mounting. When she breaks off and talks about a dream that seems to be "too big," he encourages her, telling her that if she believes in herself, she can accomplish whatever she sets her mind to do. And Jane believes him. After all, he has proved it with his life. And it all started with someone reminding him that God had a plan and that he was just the person to carry it out.

"I can truly say that I am proud to have adjusted to a handicap," Gene explained. "To do what I have done takes hard work, belief in God, and faith that he believes in me. This is something that anyone can have, handicapped or not."

Gene admits that sometimes, in the dark recesses of his mind, the impossible thought that once again he will see still lingers despite his sights being focused outward. He is in control of his life, and he likes himself.

Gene is happy and is surrounded by people he loves. Gene has reconciled his limitations without limiting his potential. He has also forgiven those who sold him short or gave up on him. He has a relationship with God that is strong, deep, and growing. He knows that God didn't desert him even at his lowest and most bitter moments. In fact, God sent an unseen woman to help the blind man see his own potential.

"I went to Vietnam with a blind heart, and I came home with unseeing eyes," he said. "I now have the ability to see with my heart, and that is so much more important, because what I have seen with my heart has allowed me to like myself and reach my dreams. I wish for others this same kind of vision."

The kind of vision that Gene has is available to all. It is a gift given by God through a messenger of faith. Gene's unseen nurse probably is responsible for many finding the path back to God and to their potential. A prayer warrior, a woman of resolve, a spiritual cheerleader, she is what every Christian can become if we choose to reach out and touch the souls who are lost and needy.

ACKNOWLEDGMENTS

I want to thank the following women of extraordinary faith for giving me their time and allowing me to include them in this volume: Dr. Anne Brooks, Helen Cornelius, Linda Davis, Mary Dunham Faulkner, Catherine Hicks, Susie Luchsinger, Marilyn Meberg, and Laurie Prange.

If you'd like to find out more about them, you can visit their websites:

http://catherinehicksonline.com/
http://lindadavis.com/
http://www.womenoffaith.com/conferences/speakers/marilyn meberg06.asp
http://www.leahssisters.org/
http://psalmsministries.com/
http://tutwilerclinic.org/
http://www.helencornelius.net/

STORIES
BEHIND
CHRISTMAS
BOXED SET
ACE COLLINS

ZONDERVAN®
.com